BECOMING A PRAYING CONGREGATION

Churchwide Leadership Tools

with Rueben P. Job

D1418260

BECOMING A PRAYING CONGREGATION
CHURCHWIDE LEADERSHIP TOOLS

ISBN 978-1-4267-0282-2

09 10 11 12 13 14 15 16 17 18—10 9 8 7 6 5 4 3 2 1
MANUFACTURED IN THE UNITED STATES OF AMERICA

CONTENTS

INTRODUCTION

Rueben P. Job

Rueben P. Job, *a retired United Methodist bishop, was formerly World Editor of The Upper Room publishing program. His previous publications include* **Three Simple Rules, A Wesleyan Spiritual Reader,** *and* **A Guide to Retreat for All God's Shepherds,** *among others. He lives in Nashville, Tennessee.*

Prayer at its best is not an additive to life; rather it is a way of living. It was so for Jesus and it may be so for us. *Becoming a Praying Congregation* is designed to bring this truth to reality in the life and ministry of your congregation and in the lives of families and individuals that make up your congregation. This way of living is nothing more or less than a constant and growing companionship with the living God made known most clearly in the life, death, and resurrection of Jesus Christ.

At their request Jesus taught the disciples how to pray and also taught them how to live a life of prayer. He walked in constant companionship with his beloved Abba and taught the disciples the essential elements of this relationship. Through the power and presence of the Holy Spirit, the wisdom and struggles of the saints of old, and the lives of the faithful and contemporary followers of Jesus we may be formed into that praying congregation, filled with praying families and individuals, walking in daily companionship with the living presence of God. To do so is to become that house of prayer (Matthew 21:13) that Jesus expected the community of faith to be and that Isaiah foretold (Isaiah 56:7).

Prayer is not an individual experience. Prayer requires two persons and so does companionship. We do not enter the experience of prayer alone or on our own. In the disciple's third experience with the resurrected Jesus (John 21) he meets them at the sea of Tiberias where the disciples had gone fishing. They had fished all night and caught nothing when Jesus told them where to fish and remarkably their nets were filled with fish. Then he asked

Prayer is not an individual experience. . . . We do not enter the experience of prayer alone or on our own.

them to bring some of the fish ashore and to have breakfast with him. Their post-resurrection experiences were just beginning but already they discovered that Jesus was still able to give direction and provide sustenance. It is something the faithful continually experience—direction and sustenance in companionship with Jesus as they begin living a life of prayer.

Richard Rohr in *Everything Belongs* has this to say about prayer: "Prayer is not primarily saying words or thinking thoughts. It is, rather, a stance. . . . It is, further, a way of living in awareness of the Presence, even enjoying the Presence. The full contemplative is not just aware of the Presence, but trusts, allows, and delights in it."[1]

When individuals, families, small groups, and entire congregations begin living in and trusting God, incredible things begin to happen. The early church reported these incredible events as signs and wonders (Acts 4:32-27; 5:12-16). The formation and transformation taking place in these early Christian communities was remarkable and gave clear witness to God's active presence and power in their midst. Grace Adolphsen Brame says, "Most of us pray that God will do something *to* us or *for* us, but God wants to do something *in* us and *through* us."[2]

God's presence and power are as available to the contemporary church as they were to the early church. *Becoming a Praying Congregation* and its companion resource, *When You Pray* (Abingdon Press, 2009), are your invitation to claim your inheritance as a follower of Christ and begin living more fully in companionship with the only One who knows you completely and loves you without limit. It is your invitation to continue or to begin the practices that will permit God to do those signs and wonders, the formation and transformation that will change and enrich your life and give witness to the world of God's active presence in your midst. It is your invitation to continue or begin those practices that will result in a lifelong companionship with God and bear the fruit of faithful discipleship, marked with joy, peace, fulfillment, confidence, and hope.

The following chapters will provide the resources you need to establish a way of living that will result in a lifetime companionship with the living and ever-present God whom we have come to know in and through Jesus Christ. The following section on "How to Use This Book" provides a pathway for you to follow. However, we also invite you to use your own creativity and use the resources offered here as you follow the guidance of the One who promised to teach us all we need to know (John 14:26). May the learning, formation, and transformation continue from this world to the next.

HOW TO USE THIS BOOK

The title of this resource presents a goal: becoming a praying congregation. Its purpose is to help you model, encourage, teach, and inspire prayer for individuals, families, and the entire congregation by providing resources and ideas that can be customized for your unique congregation. This set of tools and the process you will begin is designed to be easily modified as you continually find new ways and resources to help people grow in their spiritual practices.

Whether your community has been intentional in building and encouraging the practice of prayer for years or this is a new goal, you will find in this book a variety of ideas and tools to encourage prayer as a way of life. The materials in this resource are designed to help you:

- reach the entire congregation.
- encourage continual practice.
- help the entire congregation understand the value of a prayer practice in individual life, group life, and congregational life.
- bring prayer into all areas of church life so that prayer becomes a way of life.
- help make prayer a more integral part of worship, ministry areas, church decision making, the church's mission and witness in the world, and personal and family devotions.
- provide ongoing opportunities for all ages to learn more about prayer and the many ways to pray.
- offer simple ways to model prayer in worship and group settings.
- involve the intellect, heart, spirit, and body in prayer.
- establish a continuing churchwide practice of prayer.

There are many ways to use the ideas and resources provided here to model and encourage a practice of prayer in every area of congregational life. In addition to encouraging a personal daily prayer practice among leadership, small groups, and every member of the congregation, you can explore new ways to incorporate meaningful prayer in worship and work to develop a unifying, common language that stimulates conversation about prayer. Through small-group study, worship, preaching, and Christian education, you can help individuals to grow in their understanding of the purpose and life of prayer. You also can gain clarity about how prayer fits into the mission and decision making of the church. You will think of many other ways to use the materials provided as you seek to become a praying congregation in the coming months.

This twelve-month prayer initiative is designed to reach the entire congregation. The role of the pastor or pastors is to model, lead, and teach prayer in all aspects of church life. The role of the core leadership team, which consists of staff and/or volunteers, is to plan and oversee worship, new classes and groups, and specific ministries. The role of the congregation is to participate through worship, at-home devotional readings, and special prayer activities.

As you begin this journey, keep in mind two important and often overlooked truths about spiritual leadership:

We cannot lead others where we are unwilling to go.
We cannot be spiritual leaders without the Spirit's help.

Preparation

In the opening section, "Leading a Praying Congregation," the first steps begin with the pastor and leadership team. You cannot lead a congregation to become a prayerful community unless you are willing to enter that way of life yourself. Before beginning any churchwide focus on prayer, the pastor and leaders of the congregation must begin a personal practice of daily prayer. Together you will devote renewed focus to a daily relationship with God; discuss together the purpose, questions, and mystery of prayer; and be equipped to lead from a personal experience of prayer. The companion resource, *When You Pray*, was designed and prepared for this purpose. Based on the Revised Common Lectionary, the weekly content can become the shared source for sermon texts, group study, and personal devotions. Use it personally and in the leadership team as you prepare to lead the entire congregation in becoming a praying congregation.

To be a spiritual leader in this process of transformation, you must have the Spirit's help. True spiritual leaders must first become and then remain friends of God. As the apostle Paul wrote, "While we live, we are always being given up to death for Jesus' sake, so that the life of Jesus may be made visible in our mortal flesh" (2 Corinthians 4:11). In other words, spiritual leaders become the visible presence of Jesus in the world. John Wesley called this transforming power and presence "the image of God fresh stamped on the heart."[3] Wesley knew, as we know, that spiritual leadership is not something we do on our own; rather, it is a gift of grace that comes as we spend time with Jesus and begin to think as he thought and go where he would go. It is in this companionship with God that we are adequately formed and fed for the ministry of spiritual leadership. The ways in which God chooses to form us and feed us are as infinite as God's being and as varied and diverse as the human race.

As you begin this time of preparation through a renewed attentiveness to prayer, allow yourself time to be fed. It is easy for spiritual leaders to become so busy that there seems to be no time for personal sustenance. If we are to be spiritual leaders, we need to be fed and to rediscover those spiritually forming and transforming disciplines so that more and more the life of Jesus may be made visible in us. Wesley said, "Do justice to your own soul; give it time and means to grow. Do not starve yourself any longer."[4]

Remind yourself and your team members often that each of you is God's beloved child. Not beloved the way you once were or the way you will become. You are God's beloved now, just as you are. As you claim and live this truth for yourselves, you will be able to lead others to the wonder of this central truth.

Planning

One of the key ideas to consider as you begin to plan is the importance of building in enough time, continuity, and repetition so that prayer actually becomes a lifestyle. The primary goal or purpose of this book is to help you establish prayer as a way of living for your congregation. After all, we are not to pray for prayer's sake, but to lead us to a regular, natural, ongoing relationship with God.

Habits take time to build. In a six-week program, you have some chance of establishing new habits, but it's a tough proposition. In three months or even six months, the possibilities are greater. To truly support and develop a new way of living together, you need at least one year. The sample plans provided here outline how you might use the ideas in this book, and in the companion resource *When You Pray*, to develop new habits over the next twelve months. At the end of this year of learning and living as a praying community you will be prepared for a lifetime of continuing growth in your relationship with God.

First, consider your plan for getting started. Feel free to adapt the following plan to meet your unique situation and needs.

Getting Started

Activity		Duration
Begin, continue, or refocus a personal prayer practice.	Before assembling a leadership group to work with you, begin or revitalize your own daily prayer practice. Listen for God's guidance in your planning.	2–4 weeks
Identify a team.	As you are revitalizing your own prayer practice, begin to look for at least two or three other people (or more) to form a leadership team. This group will work with you to consider planning and teaching for the entire congregation.	Same 2–4 weeks
Have team members begin a personal prayer practice.	As a group, begin the practice of personal prayer, preferably using *When You Pray* or some other resource, such as *A Guide to Prayer for All Who Seek God* (Upper Room, 2006) or *A Wesleyan Spiritual Reader* (Abingdon, 1998). Meet weekly to share your experiences.	4 weeks
Take a prayer retreat.	Plan a retreat, whether for an afternoon or for several days. During this time together, resist talking about programs and strategies. Instead, spend time in prayer and talk deeply about your understanding of prayer and your questions about prayer. (See page 50 for a helpful guide to retreat.)	End of same 4 weeks
As a team, outline and commit to your goals.	Plan together the goals you have for the next three, six, and twelve months. (See the action plan examples that follow this plan.)	2–4 weeks (Post-retreat)

Setting Goals

As you and your team set goals for the year, begin by asking yourself questions such as these:

- What areas are most important in the next twelve months?
- What changes or new steps will we take in these areas?
- Who do we want to reach?
- With what groups or settings will we begin?
- How will we know if we are successful?
- Will this plan repeat each season or year?

You may determine to makes changes or take new steps in areas such as:

- Life of your leadership
- Church decision making
- Worship
- Children and youth
- Encouraging family prayer
- Adult Sunday school and small groups

As you set goals together, be as specific as possible. It is better to have a more modest goal if it is a goal that you can describe, assign responsibility for, and define what a successful result would look like. Here is a sample goal outline:

Goal: We will become a praying congregation at home.

What	Who	When	Results
1. List what you'd like to do and the steps, in order, to accomplish it.	Who will lead? Who can help?	When will you begin? When are the beginning and concluding times for each step?	What is the result of this plan?
Example:			
1. Help each parent in the congregation encourage children in prayer at home.	Christian Education Committee	Begin after Easter Sunday	At least 30 families participate in small-group activities
A. Distribute the handout "Parents Teaching Children to Pray" (on DVD-Rom).	John Smith	Easter Sunday and the following Sunday in all worship services	Follow-up contact with selection of families
B. Offer two intergenerational Wednesday evening workshops on prayer.	Jane and John Doe	Second and third Wednesdays in May	Collect ideas and volunteers to improve the plan for next year
Follow-up: Plan to offer this help for families during the next calendar year.			

Creating Your One-Year Plan

As you create a full plan for the year ahead, be sure to cycle your efforts and activities through every aspect of congregational life—from the worship service and small groups to plans for individuals and families at home. Allow time for checking in with your leadership team to ask questions about what the experience has been thus far, where change has been observed, and where the obstacles have come.

Feel free to use the following sample one-year plan or adapt it as you wish to meet the needs of your particular congregation. (Note: The following chart is available on the DVD-Rom to print and customize.)

Activity	Instruction	Duration
Begin prayer and preparation	The pastor/s and staff begin a renewed daily prayer practice using *When You Pray*.	Months 1 & 2 (8-week duration)
Form leadership team	Identify two or more key leaders who can join the pastor and/or staff to form a leadership team. (Consider groups/leaders such as spiritual formation committee, administrative board, key Sunday school class or small group.)	Month 1
Leadership team begins renewed daily prayer practice	Invite leadership team to join you in using *When You Pray*.	Month 2 (4-week duration)
Hold prayer retreat	Take the leadership team on a prayer retreat for several hours, a day, or longer. Spend time discussing the meaning of prayer, questions about prayer, and personal prayer practices and experiences.	End of Month 2 Read Rueben Job's helpful guide to retreat (page 50) for ideas.
Set goals	With the leadership team, identify and outline your goals for the next three, six, and twelve months.	Month 3 (Post-retreat)
Plan sermon series	Work with your worship planners to schedule a sermon series.	Months 3 & 4 (4–6-week duration)

One-Year Plan continued . . .		
Focus on worship	Work with your worship team to identify one or two changes you can make in the service that will help people encounter God in worship.	Month 4 See K. C. Ptomey's article on silence and liturgy, "All of Worship as Prayer," on page 74. Pamela Hawkins' article on "Modeling Prayer on Worship's Main Stage" (page 69) explores how people are invited into prayer.
Launch *When You Pray*, encouraging the congregation in personal prayer	Invite the congregation to begin using *When You Pray* as a daily prayer guide. During your sermon series, present the book and lift up the themes used in the series. Share quotes in the bulletin or newsletter each week for three weeks to introduce the congregation to the book. Once the books are distributed, find ways through testimonies from your leadership team, references in worship, or articles on your church website to talk about the experience of daily prayer and to continue lifting up quotes. Seeing references to words from their daily practice will be a unifying experience for the congregation.	Month 4 Read the article "Creating Space for Authentic Living Creates Space for Authentic Prayer Lives" by Connie and Joseph Shelton on page 99.
Begin small-group study	As individuals begin a daily prayer practice, suggest a six-week emphasis on *When You Pray* among Sunday school classes, small groups, women's groups, and men's groups. Committing to a daily prayer practice as a group may help members to adopt the habit. (A leader guide, *When You Pray as a Small Group*, is available for those who want session plans.)	Months 5 & 6 (6-week duration) Explore Laurie Barnes' article on "15 Ways to Pray in a Small Group" on page 160 (also on DVD-Rom) for ideas to share with group leaders.

One-Year Plan continued . . .		
Reflect	Meet with your leadership team and ask: • What are we seeing? • What changes have taken place? • What needs more attention? Don't be discouraged. If the team doesn't sense any change, take a collective look at worship. Consider inviting at least two committed small groups to begin using *When You Pray*. Ask for their help.	Month 6 Are you reaching the diverse members of your congregation? Read Nancy C. Reeves' article, "Prayer for All Personality Types," on page 147. Think about where obstacles lie in prayer formation. Kim Thomas, on page 79, describes a return to simplicity for her congregation.
Make time for the children and their prayers in worship	With your children's teachers and worship team, work to include the children in special moments in worship.	Barbara Davis' article on children's prayer time in worship on page 93 may offer ideas to your team.
Consult with Administrative Board/ other decision making group	Work with the leaders of your congregation's board or leadership group to find ways to begin meetings with a time of meaningful prayer.	Month 7 Read K. C. Ptomey's story on beginning meetings with prayer on page 40. Share Tyrone Gordon's excerpt from *F.O.C.U.S.* on page 45 with your board.
Plan an emphasis on children/teens and prayer	Explore new ways to teach children/teens about prayer; introduce creative prayer methods and tools; and equip parents, grandparents, Sunday school teachers, and others for encouraging children/teens to . . . *(cont. next page)*	Share and discuss Leanne Ciampa Hadley's "Prayer and Children" (page 135), and "Teens and Prayer" . . . *(cont. next page)*

One-Year Plan continued . . .		
	. . . pray. You might have a special study or emphasis on prayer for children and youth during the month, as well as involve children/youth in worship. Consider having a prayer event designed especially for children or youth.	. . . (page 141) with your children's, youth, and leadership teams.
Reaching young adults	Plan a prayer experience for young adults. Try experiential prayer stations, media meditation (see the prayer loops on the DVD-Rom), or an online interactive prayer site.	Sally Dyck's method of using beads as a prayer ritual on page 156 has been very popular with 20-somethings. Ben Simpson's article on prayer and the Internet offers ways to begin to connect online (page 116).
Encourage praying couples	Host a "Praying Couples" class. (Class session outlines and materials for couples to use at home are provided on the DVD-Rom.) Find a setting for couples and more experienced mentors to meet and share their experiences a few weeks later.	Month 8 (2-week class; 15-week duration) Laurie Barnes and Shirley Yarick provide curriculum for "Praying Couples" on the DVD-Rom.
Reflect on your progress	Meet with your leadership team and ask again: • What are we seeing? • What changes have taken place? • What needs more attention? • What groups within the life of the church will we lift up as our focus for the next few months?	Month 9 Stacy Hood shares three experiential activities for worship in her article "Experiential Prayer in Worship" on page 87.

One-Year Plan continued . . .		
Equip families for prayer at home	Encourage families to pray together at home. Plan a sermon on the importance of spiritual instruction and leadership in the home. Consider holding a class or workshop for parents and other caregivers on how to teach children to pray and how to lead prayer in the home.	Read "Encouraging Praying House-holds" (page 163), "Praying at Home" (page 170), and "Parents Teaching Children to Pray" (page 178). A family devotional guide, *When You Pray as a Family*, is available for those who would like plans and ideas for family devotions.
Prayer event	Plan and hold a special prayer event that invites participation from the entire congregation. Consider inviting individuals, leaders/staff, and/or groups to share experiences and observations from recent weeks at this event or in worship during the month.	Month 10 Andy Langford's article on "Healing Services" (page 111) may offer ideas for special emphases.
Reach out to others	Prayer and service are a natural partnership. Work with your missions committee—or a new group eager to begin—to set aside a time of prayer about your community and world. Look for new ways to offer aid and comfort.	Month 11 Andy Langford's article on prayer shawls on page 114 tells a story of tangible signs of prayer. Stacy Hood's church assembled mission kits during morning worship; see article on page 87.
Celebrate your journey	Meet as a leadership team and look back on the year. Recognize the accomplishments and the new areas of vitality in a public way— testimonials from lay leaders, couples and families, recognizing small groups, celebrating the journey of children and youth.	Month 12

Continuing the Journey

Just as prayer is a lifelong journey for each individual, so it is a continual journey for each congregation. If you are like most congregations, you may have the experience of needing a fresh start at some point during the year. At the end of this book you will find a section called "Living as a Praying Congregation," which includes ideas for re-launching your efforts at any time as well as ideas for subsequent years.

Additional resources to support your prayer emphasis are discussed on pages 19–20.

Overview of the Sections

This resource includes several broad areas of topics and ideas including:

I. Leading a Praying Congregation

As the spiritual leaders of a congregation, a prayerful pastor and leadership team are absolutely integral to the prayer life of a church. In this section, you and your team will:
- Explore the role of the pastor in leading prayer and read personal experiences of clergy and lay leaders.
- Look at the value of the personal prayer life of the pastor as well as the importance of the pastoral prayer and see some examples.
- Examine prayer as a way of living the gospel of Jesus Christ—prayer as a lifestyle, not simply something we do.

II. Making Prayer Central in Worship

Worship services are one of the most visible doors of entry for visitors into the life of the congregation. Whenever we gather for worship, worship is also one of the best opportunities for guidance and teaching about a life of prayer. In this section, you and your team will:
- Identify the ways and places prayer is taught or modeled well in your worship service.
- Imagine how newcomers experience and participate in your service and look for ways to welcome and guide them.
- Make a thorough and deep exploration of the ways your worship experience helps people encounter God.

III. The Congregation in Prayer

Though they sometimes differ in the methods, every congregation should provide for members and visitors a welcoming atmosphere where they can freely receive and offer prayer. As you consider the prayer ministry your church currently offers and how it can be renewed and improved, you and your team will:

- Discover ways congregations can emphasize prayer in the various elements of their life together.
- Consider practical instruction on handling prayer requests and the use of social media tools in expanding prayer communities.
- Find helpful outlines for finding and training volunteers in prayer ministry.

IV. Teaching Prayer Practices With Children, Youth, and Adults

One of the most important roles of the church is to teach and encourage a life of prayer for all ages. Providing a variety of prayer practices for different age groups and personality types ensures that everyone receives the instruction and encouragement he or she needs. As you reflect on the prayer practices of your church, you and your team will:

- Review and outline the focus of prayer instruction in your church.
- Look carefully at the ways you currently help different age groups develop a relationship with God through prayer.
- Think through the variety of prayer forms and experiences your church offers and consider their appeal to both introverts and extroverts.

V. Becoming a Praying Congregation at Home

Only when families are living a life of prayer outside the church walls does prayer truly become a vital part of what happens within the church. Equipping families to become praying households is crucial. In this section, you will consider questions such as:

- How does your congregation encourage and facilitate prayer in the home?
- Practically speaking, how do you equip parents and other caregivers to teach and model prayer at home?
- What are you doing to encourage couples to pray together on a regular basis?

VI. Living as a Praying Congregation

Establishing a real and growing companionship with God is a lifelong journey for each individual, family, and congregation. This section provides practical tools for sustaining and enriching the journey through the first year and beyond, as you consider questions such as:

- What are some of the potential challenges we face as we seek to sustain a yearlong emphasis on prayer?
- How can we target specific groups and segments within the congregation in our planning, communication, and implementation of activities and events?
- How can we help our congregation to continue growing and maturing in a life of prayer after the first twelve months?

About the Companion Resource

When You Pray: Daily Practices for Prayerful Living
by Rueben P. Job

When You Pray is a thoughtful guide that explores the daily practices of living a prayerful life. This resource, with weekly themes and daily Scripture, can provide a consistent connection through the year to draw leaders, small groups, and the whole congregation into a shared experience of prayer practice.

This excellent resource designed for use in a daily prayer time responds to the need we all have for a pattern of prayer that is accessible, usable, and adaptable to our diverse life experiences. Based on the pattern of prayer Jesus gave his disciples, the weekly readings provide ancient and contemporary resources that help lead the reader to a closer relationship with God. Each week's theme and Scripture selections are drawn from the three-year lectionary, with a variety of quotations and an original essay by Bishop Rueben Job providing additional insights related to each week's theme. A bibliography lists additional resources for further spiritual reading.

Churches participating in *Becoming a Praying Congregation* will benefit from using *When You Pray* in a variety of ways:

Pastor
- Use the book to renew your own practice of daily prayer and prepare for the churchwide prayer emphasis.
- Turn to the theme, Scripture, essay, and quotes to build content for a 4–6-week sermon series.

Church Staff and Leadership Team
- Invite the staff and leadership team to use the book as a daily prayer resource. Share experiences and insights in a prayer retreat following this period.
- Invite members of the staff and leadership team to share testimonies of their personal experiences in using *When You Pray* in worship, at a special prayer event, or through newsletter or website articles.
- Share quotes in the bulletin or newsletter to introduce the congregation to the book.

Small Groups
- Invite adult Sunday school classes and other small groups to use the book individually and collectively for a 4–6-week study. A leader guide, *When You Pray as a Small Group*, is available for those who want session plans.

Individual Members / Households

- Offer *When You Pray* as a daily prayer guide for each household in the congregation.
- Provide quotes and articles related to the book in the newsletter or on the church website. Seeing references to words from their daily practice will serve as a unifying act for the congregation.

Families

- Encourage families to use *When You Pray* as a tool for family devotions. A family devotional guide, *When You Pray as a Family*, is available for those who would like devotional plans and ideas.

I.
LEADING A PRAYING CONGREGATION

Prayer is an essential part of an ongoing relationship with God. This truth applies not only to individuals but to congregations as well. As the spiritual leaders of a congregation, a prayerful pastor and leadership team are absolutely integral to the prayer life of a church. Keeping prayer at the forefront of all aspects of ministry is key to these roles. In this section, you will explore the role of the pastor in leading prayer and read personal experiences of clergy and lay leaders as you:

- Consider how prayer gives voice to the role of the pastor and identify the pastor as prayer guide to the congregation.
- Understand the importance of pastoral prayer—as a vocal prayer of intercession for the congregation and the community and of thanksgiving and dependence on God.
- Look at the value of the personal prayer life of the pastor as it enables the pastor to be renewed and rely more fully on God.
- Examine prayer as a way of living the gospel of Jesus Christ—prayer as a lifestyle, not simply something we do.
- Read how the prayer practices of another faith helped one church leader understand better her ability to "pray without ceasing."
- Explore the prayer practices of Jesus and the early church, learn how to model these in today's congregations, and see an example of a daily prayer service.

Articles:

THE PASTOR ROLE IN THE PRAYER LIFE OF THE CHURCH

Pamela Hawkins

Pamela Hawkins *is the editor of* **Weavings,** *a quarterly journal that promotes a pattern of faithful living through prayer, community, and engagement. Pam is also an ordained United Methodist pastor. In this article, she describes prayer as that which gives voice to the role of pastor. Pam examines how the pastor is prayer guide to the congregation, one who leads God's people into a deepening life of prayer.*

Pastor for the first time in my first congregation, I sat down to prepare for Sunday's worship and was caught off guard by prayer in my new role. Fresh out of seminary training and seasoned by years of churchgoing, I had expected to feel ready to lead God's people. Yet, as I reviewed my congregation's order of worship, I counted seven different public prayers with my name assigned to them. I still recall the wave of anxiety that rose up in the pit of my stomach. I had been taught about preaching and teaching. I had taken classes in ethics, theology, pastoral counseling, and polity. But the ministry of prayer had rarely found its way into a class outline or official practicum of my pastoral preparation. Yet, there it was, in the black and white expectation of my first leadership task. Prayer was everywhere: a Call to Worship; prayers of confession, intercession, and two of silence; there were the pastoral prayer and The Prayer of Great Thanksgiving at the Lord's Table—all mine to lead while my fellow pastor, in the same liturgy, was responsible for a prayer of illumination, the prayers of baptism, and the benediction. In ways I had not consciously anticipated nor been attentive to before, prayer illumined and expressed the role of pastor as leader.

While I have spent much of my life engaged as a praying layperson in the church in a variety of ministries—Sunday school, youth mission trips, weekly worship services, Bible studies, congregational prayer vigils—when approaching prayer as a new pastor, I sensed a difference. There was a fresh responsibility and weight carried in both words and silence; there was a new significance to body language and intent, even to belief about prayer. For all the prayers through which others had

In ways I had not consciously anticipated nor been attentive to before, prayer illumined and expressed the role of pastor as leader.

led me over the course of my life, never before had I consciously considered the importance of the pastor's role in prayer. I simply took their prayers for granted.

But once I became a pastor, my awareness changed and my eyes opened to how much it had meant to me, over those years, when my pastors had attended to prayer with clear intent, transparent vulnerability, and careful preparation. Equally significant, I came to understand, were those experiences of prayer led by pastors for whom prayer seemed to be simply punctuation or necessity; something to do or get through. Even in those first few moments of pastoral leadership, I knew deep within me which kind of leader I longed to become in the prayer life of God's people. I knew, because the One who called me and who calls all pastors to this set apart and demanding role, longs for us to recognize and elevate prayer's significance in the relationship between God and God's people. I agree with fellow pastor Marjorie Thompson that "prayer is the essential expression of this relationship," it expresses how "God relates to us and how we in turn relate to God." I also resonate with her words, "the health and vitality of this relationship depend on clarity and frequency of communication."[5] In other words, to become a praying person or congregation, to "attune ourselves to the conversation already going on deep in our hearts," to "align our conscious intentions with the desire of God being expressed at our core," will require time, attention, and commitment—commitment that does not rest solely on the pastor's shoulders, but a "mutual commitment"[6] among God, pastor, and congregation.

It has taken time for me, as I imagine it has for many other pastors, to find my footing as a leader in congregational prayer. It has taken time, trials and errors, and much mentoring. In those first shaky days as "pastor," with the mantle of leadership barely touching my shoulders, my prayer memory flickered, as if I had prayer-amnesia, or more accurately, prayer-apraxia, an inability to perform the prayers that had, throughout my life, made a home in my heart. The lens and role of leadership can do this to a person—cause us to see the familiar as completely new; to put on "old-hat" habits as if never before worn. And when the leadership threshold we are called to cross is from congregant to pastor, then the words "let us pray" become our words to lead and teach. Pastors are not, of course, the only prayer leaders in a congregation. In every hallway, office, kitchen, classroom, and worship space, people of prayer help others learn to pray, lay and clergy alike. But the particular role and responsibility of a pastor to lead a congregation in prayer cannot be denied, delayed, or defused. We become a guide to prayer when we become a pastor. We become a guide to a journey every human heart has already begun, on a path where previous generations have left their mark, and in a direction illumined by the Holy Spirit that all might find our way.

> **The particular role and responsibility of a pastor to lead a congregation in prayer cannot be denied, delayed, or defused. We become a guide to prayer when we become a pastor.**

How heartening and essential it is, then, for pastors to remember that the responsibility for the prayer life of a congregation does not begin or end with us; rather, we join in, illumine, behold, shape, carve, lift up, connect, put voice to, and hold the prayers that God and God's people long to share. At the same time, with a pastor's yes to God's prayerful call comes the pastor's yes to leading God's people into a deepening life of prayer, a role that cannot be taken for granted, carelessly prepared, or treated as secondary to other ministries. On any given day, prayer will be the ministry in which a pastor will most often serve as leader. From early morning hospital visits to mid-morning Bible studies to midday counseling sessions; from community prayer gatherings to personal moments of solitude; from nursery to nursing home; from funeral to rehearsal dinner; privately, with two or three, and in standing-room-only crowds; pastors are called upon to help congregations become praying congregations. The sheer volume and repetition of prayerful expectations in the life of a pastor, combined with all the other leadership accountabilities of the role, can dry out mouth and heart, causing our prayers to seem "careless and slovenly" in their expression.[7] It is not uncommon, with the relentless press on time and spirit, for a pastor to fall prey to taking the ministry of prayer for granted as the prayerful words of another pastor remind us:

> **On any given day, prayer will be the ministry in which a pastor will most often serve as leader. From early morning hospital visits to midday counseling sessions . . . from nursery to nursing home . . . pastors are called upon to help congregations become praying congregations.**

> O, Lord, you have to catch me on the run most of the time.
> I am too busy to stop,
>   too important to pause for contemplation.
> I hold up too big a section of the sky
>   to sit down and meditate.[8]

How, then, whether at the beginning or mid-stream of our vocation as pastor, are we to get our bearings and keep them as leaders for praying congregations? Perhaps the best place to start, and return to at any time along the pastoral way, is the source and beginning of our call itself. Is it not through prayer that God calls pastors to become leaders? Is it not through prayer that pastors wrestle with, debate, resist, delight in, and respond to this call? God calls leaders out of and into prayer (1 Samuel 3:1-18; Psalm 139; Isaiah 6:1-9a; Luke 9:1-6; Acts 9:10-19; Romans 8:26-27). Pastoral leadership begins in prayer. There God names us, makes a home in us, stirs about and waits in us until, in prayer, we respond yes or no to the call, not just once, but time and again. And when a prayerful yes is first given back to God, that yes becomes an act of pastoral leadership—a pastor's first "prayer of the people"—a prayer rising from and returning to the people of God. A pastor's yes to the role and responsibility to which God calls is both a prayer of thanksgiving and a prayer of petition; a word of gratitude for what is and a cry for help for what will be needed to faithfully lead a congregation.

And help will always be there, if we will seek and accept it, connecting pastor and people with the One in whom all of our prayers find their beginning and their end. Help will always be there, for pastor and congregation, because God's prayers are steadfast and unending, an unceasing source and resource for pastoral leadership. And because we have never been and will never be alone in our prayers: we, as pastors, are surrounded not only by a great cloud of prayerful witnesses, but also by an extended family of prayerful companions. We are co-laborers, co-creators, co-authors of congregational prayer. But as pastors, we have a set-apart charge to help our congregations connect with God, and all that God loves, through prayer. It is our charge to guide our congregations so that they might see, feel, make, and trust the connection between God's life and our lives, between the holy and the everyday, "between heaven and earth, . . . this world and the next, the invisible and the visible."[9] This is the work and promise of prayer; no small feat, to say the least. But then, prayer is not about saying the least, it is about communicating "the most precious expression of being human" with the very One who made us.[10] Prayer gives voice to the role of pastor.

Ideas to Consider

- Pam describes the feelings of anxiety she experienced the first Sunday with her first congregation as a pastor just out of seminary. As a pastor or church leader, have you felt a similar inexperience with "the ministry of prayer"?
- Pam says that while pastors are not the only prayer leaders in a congregation, pastors do have a "set-apart charge" as guides to prayer.

PERSONAL PRAYER IN THE LIFE OF THE PASTOR

Pamela Hawkins

Pamela Hawkins *is the editor of* **Weavings,** *a quarterly journal that promotes a pattern of faithful living through prayer, community, and engagement. Pam is also an ordained United Methodist pastor. Here, Pam discusses the necessity of personal prayer in the life of a pastor and offers three practices that have deepened her own prayer life.*

When all else fails, or seems to fail, I pray. Sermons come and go; church programs rise and fall; vision is clear, then cloudy; but prayer, the prayer of my life as a pastor and a person, is unceasing, outpouring, and sustaining, without fail. I have not always known this to be true, but have learned it from others who share my call. In the early days of my call to ministry, I did not recognize personal prayer as the life-giving spiritual practice that it is. This is a truth I have learned to appreciate, and to lean into, like drought-thirsty leaves lean into overdue rain. It has taken time, as a pastor, to discover that prayer, personal prayer, is what keeps my heart from hardening and my life open to the "Holy Spirit" who "must live in the bloodstream" of those called to lead God's people in life together.[11]

These discoveries about personal prayer have not been self-discoveries. As I look back over the course of ministry, when I close my eyes and recall how each form of prayer that I have claimed were introduced to me, I see the faces and hear the prayers of others who have taught me to pray. This is not to say that the capacity and practice of prayer were not already and always at work in me, as it is, I believe, in all persons, but rather that my personal prayer life has been shaped and affirmed by people whose prayers attracted and attended to me. What I now know, believe, and practice about prayer I have not learned on my own. Prayer, like a cherished family story, is handed down; passed along; taught from generation to generation; whispered from sister to sister; shared from father to son. And as it is passed along, prayer takes form and shape from the personal life of the one who prays—our memories, our needs, our longings, our call, our life.

In other words: The personal prayer life of a pastor is just this—personal. Here is one part of our work that can be nothing but, and needs not to be anything more than, completely between us and the One who calls us. So much of a pastor's spiritual life must be molded around the needs and spiritual life of a congregation; but

Too often, pastors are lured into a false belief that for the sake of time and energy, the spiritual practices we lead for others will be sufficient for our own spiritual vitality.

personal prayer is about the needs and spiritual life of the person of pastor. Too often, pastors are lured into a false belief that for the sake of time and energy, the spiritual practices we lead for others will be sufficient for our own spiritual vitality. Congregational prayers can contain our prayers, congregational grief can contain our grief, congregational retreat can contain brief moments of our retreat, at least in-between the leadership and hospitality commitments that we make, as pastor. And there is surely some truth in this: A pastor's life, in every dimension, intersects and is woven through the life of a congregation. But a truth that is equally, if not more rooted in our call is that a pastor's life must stay intersected with and woven through the life of God. For my own pastoral life, it has

been through practices of personal prayer that my life and God's life have been most strongly held together. Let me share three practices that have grown in importance to my personal prayer life, each of which I have learned from someone whose life intersected and influenced my own by the grace of God.

A pastor's life must stay intersected with and woven through the life of God.

Praying With Assurance

In 1994 I learned that I had been using a prayer book every week for most of my life and had never known it. At that time I was a second-career pastor-in-training, mother of a grade-schooler and college student, settling into my first seminary field education placement, and trying keep up with my full-time "other" job at a university. In a conversation with my supervisor, I shared that one of my goals for the semester was to learn more about prayer. Self-consciously, I told him that beyond the Lord's Prayer and the prayers of confession printed in the worship bulletin of our church, I did not feel like I knew how to pray very well, yet I felt drawn to prayer. I wanted some kind of instruction book or handout.

After listening to my request, he turned to the bookshelf beside his desk, searched for a few moments, then pulled a single book to his lap and held it there for me to see. I knew the book. I had used it for years. I did not own a copy, but before he even opened it, I could recall bits and pieces of words spread across its pages. With no note of judgment or impatience, he asked, "Have you used this prayer book?" He held a copy of the hymnal of my tradition; the same book I shared with my parents, husband, children, and friends in worship settings, Bible studies, and other congregational gatherings for most of my life. It was the book of my childhood, into which I had slipped scraps of paper, proudly marking each hymn because I could read numbers. It was the book of my youth, from which I read when I was confirmed in the church. It was the book of my young adulthood, from which we read prayers when our children were baptized, when our friends were married, and when our parents were buried. It was the book from which I had joined my voice with hundreds of others during Advent, Christmas, Lent, and Easter, finding instruction, lyrics, words, and guidance throughout its pages. I knew this book. But not until then had I had ever recognized it as a prayer book for my life.

To this day, and almost every day, I use prayer books of all kinds to guide my personal prayer. For me, the availability, traditions, and resources of prayers from across time are prayers of assurance. I am reassured in my own prayers by the words, images, rhythms, stories, and movements that precede me. My prayers are reassured through printed resources and oral traditions beyond me. My prayers join in the prayers of creation, of generations, of voices that span God's history with humanity. This was no small learning for me. Without my mentor's reassuring example that the prayers of my life were already undergirded and illumined by the prayers of a community, I might have remained prayerfully self-conscious and uncertain. As a pastor, I have often found myself on the other side of the same self-conscious conversation, where someone in my congregation longs for some tangible guide to prayer. In gratitude, I try to share with them what has been shared with me.

As a pastor, I have often found myself on the other side of the same self-conscious conversation, where someone in my congregation longs for some tangible guide to prayer. In gratitude, I try to share with them what has been shared with me.

Praying With Integrity

In the quiet candlelit darkness, the congregation waits. Opening songs have been sung and daily Scriptures, read—silent space has been given for music and Word to settle into the lives of the gathered community. The pastor stands and slowly moves to the front of the worship space. She begins to lead the pastoral prayer. People come for this; they say so, they invite others to come too, to experience this pastor's prayers because—"prayer really happens here." Something "shows" in the prayers of this woman. Something becomes available that people want, long for, absorb, receive, memorize, and trust.

I have the privilege of friendship with this pastor. So I know that when she prays and I am the only one around, her prayers have the same special, inviting quality. I am just as drawn to her prayers when we are the only two praying, as when I am seated with a hundred other people in the congregation. I have no doubt that when she is alone in prayer, the nature of her prayer is no different. My friend prays in a way where access to God is believable and present; she prays in a way where feelings for and about God can happen, are invited and encouraged. I have asked her about her prayers; about why she thinks it is that people are drawn to pray with her in such powerful and dramatic ways.

Her response says it all for me: "I believe, really believe, that God wants to listen to our prayers. I believe something happens here, that this prayer is real."

And she does. My friend believes in prayer, and it shows. There is integrity about her prayers, integrity that begins in her personal prayer life and carries through the public prayers she leads. She believes that prayer aligns her heart with God's heart; she believes that her prayers matter to God and that God's prayers matter for her. When she is praying in the midst of the congregation, I believe it is integrity that creates what people sense: prayer happens because there is a deeply held conviction by the one who prays that prayer really matters. I find this way of prayer to be contagious, as do many people who have prayed with this pastor. My friend's integrity, her deep belief in the value of what she prays, has influenced my prayer life to its very core and I seek to pray in ways that align my heart with the heart of God so that my belief in prayer is evident too. I believe that prayer matters, and I seek to grow in prayerful, honest integrity as I live the life of pastor.

Praying With Openness

In the back corner on the second floor of the church my mother attended for over fifty years there is a prayer room. It is a beautiful room, well decorated and softly lit so that those who come to pray or study can do so comfortably. Icons and candles adorn tables and a large reproduction of Rembrandt's painting of "The Return of the Prodigal Son" hangs on one wall, along with a small plaque that informs any reader that the room is dedicated in honor and memory of my mother.

If a visitor to the church inquires about the connection between that prayer room and my mother, they would be told that it is because of her dedication to prayer. She was, in fact, a praying presence in the life of that congregation, as well as in the life of her family. People knew about her daily prayers; her tiny spiral-bound prayer journals; her quiet, persistent intercessions. Rarely public in her prayers, her private prayers were sought, requested, and trusted by people of all ages within that congregation and beyond.

My mother never tired of prayer, and she was always open to the Spirit's leading in the prayers of her life. She was open to praying in new ways and with new people. It was not uncommon for her to intentionally join a small group study where most members were twenty years or more her junior and where prayer was a guiding spiritual practice of the study sessions. Often, when presented with opportunities to experience unfamiliar prayers like those of Taizé or for healing and wholeness or with a Benedictine community of monks, my mother would be one of the first to sign up, even in her last years when she first became ill.

What I have acquired from my mother's personal prayer life into my own is a lifelong openness to the movement and presence of the Holy Spirit through the gift of prayer. My mother taught me about prayers of openness. She taught me to experiment, take risks, watch for clues, change my ways, ask for help, and ride the winds of grace and gratitude that breeze through my personal prayer life whether I am ready for them or not. And ready or not, my personal prayer life as a pastor will forever be shaped and formed by what my mother taught me through her prayers of openness and her openness to prayer.

Before writing this article about personal prayer in the life of the pastor, I almost headed in a different direction. I considered, and even began to make, a list and description of prayer practices that have "stuck" with me in my personal life—like breath prayers, labyrinth prayers, a daily office, and the prayer of examen. But then, even for me, even for now, the list would be, in part, a moving target. And for anyone who read my list, the prayers of their own lives would not be represented or included. So I have tried, instead, to describe some of what I have learned through my personal prayer life. I know that for every pastor, the forms of prayer

Our personal prayers take flight and life from our personal relationship with God.

that enrich and enliven our life with God and our passion for ministry will vary from one person to the next. I know that the forms of prayer that catch our attentive hearts and nourish our creative spirits may not be the same as those desired by the congregation we lead or by our closest colleague or mentor. Our personal prayers take flight and life from our personal relationship with God; and like relationships, they will change, deepen, challenge, sweeten, struggle, morph, seem to disappear and then reappear out of the blue. Prayer, like vocabulary and technology, changes over time according to circumstance, geography, discovery, and creative collaboration between the Holy Spirit and the human spirit. But what does not change, and will not change, is the open, love-aligning, reassuring heart of God from which all our prayers extend and to which all our prayers return.

Ideas to Consider

- Consider Pam's assessment that pastors too often rely on the spiritual practices they lead others in to sustain themselves spiritually. How has a personal prayer life sustained and strengthened you to lead others?
- Pam shares three practices of a personal prayer life, each learned from prayerful people in her life. What have you learned from those in your life who pray faithfully? What wisdom might you share with someone struggling in his or her personal prayer life?

THE PASTORAL PRAYER

Joe E. Pennel

Joe E. Pennel *served as a pastor in local churches in Memphis and Nashville over a period of thirty years. In 1996 Pennel was assigned Bishop of the Virginia Conference of The United Methodist Church where he served for eight years. Now retired, he continues to serve as the Professor of Pastoral Leadership and is a published author. In this article, Pennel enunciates the importance of the pastoral prayer as speaking on behalf of the congregation and drawing the people into the presence of God.*

Vocal prayer makes a bold assumption. It embraces the conviction that God is living, active, and present in the lives of individuals and in the life of the congregation. It holds to the belief that ours is not an absent God. It assumes our absolute dependence on this God who is far beyond us and deep within us. So, the pastoral prayer is offered to a God who is current, relational, and participatory. If the pastor is not so convicted, the pastoral prayer will not benefit the congregation's deep yearning for the soul of God.

I was elected to the episcopacy in The United Methodist Church in 1996 and since that time have worshipped in over five hundred congregations. Most of these have had a pastoral prayer as one part of the service of worship. Some of these have drawn me into the presence of God but many of them have not. It is not difficult to fail worshippers at the point of the pastoral prayer.

Paul, a pastor friend of mine traveled to a nearby state park every Friday morning to prepare the pastoral prayer for the following Sunday morning. His preparation of the pastoral prayer grew out of his awareness of the spiritual and temporal needs of his congregation and of his perception of what was going on in the world at that particular time. He would muse prayer and write as he sat at a picnic table overlooking the wide and winding Tennessee River. He spent time in prayer before he prepared the prayer. In following this discipline he did not disregard the importance of the pastoral prayer. I have not followed his example, but I wish that I had.

My confession is that I have not taken seriously the notion that my congregations have trusted me to formulate a prayer that would enable the worshippers to be attentive to God's presence. Sunday in and Sunday out I relied too heavily on spontaneity and vague generalities. This led to prayers that did not plow deeply into the needs of the people whom I had been appointed to serve. I would often use well-worn clichés that I read from my memory bank. As I review this part of my ministry, my public prayers were not much more than a formality and I am not proud of this.

Pastoral prayer is *oratio*: praying with words. In vocal prayer, we use spoken words to express thanksgiving and dependence on God, intercede for those in the congregation, pray for the community in which the church is located, pray for the church family, confess our sins, express penitence, and to adore God for being God.

Sunday in and Sunday out I relied too heavily on spontaneity and vague generalities. This leads to prayers that did not plow deeply into the needs of the people whom I had been appointed to serve.

"Out of the depths I cry to you, O LORD." (Psalm 130:1)

Vocal prayer, on behalf of the congregation, should be filled with words that come from the heart. The heart will be directed to God if the pastoral prayer comes from the depths of the pastor's soul. If the prayer is not from the heart, it will not be sincere. The pastoral prayer that does not come from the heart cannot lift the hearts of others to God. If the *oratio* does not come from the heart, it will fill the sanctuary from wall to wall and from floor to ceiling with empty words that will not open persons to the presence of the Holy. If the pastoral prayer is truly from the heart, it will help the worshippers to be drawn into the presence of God. When this happens, the congregation is better able to strengthen its hold on truth, goodness, righteousness, purity, and love. Prayers that are not from the heart will not accomplish that purpose.

1. **The pastoral prayer should be thoughtful and well prepared.** The prayer does not begin when the pastor faces the bowed heads of the congregation. It has its birth in the prayer life of the pastor. A wise rabbi was asked, "What does the rabbi do before praying?" He answered, "I pray that I might be able to pray properly."

2. **It is important to give careful preparation.** Words have power. Words can make this look like that. They can heal or they can hurt, build up or tear down, and they can shape reality. They can be used to point to the one who is praying or they can point beyond the prayer to that which is Holy. Well chosen words have the strength to draw worshippers into the presence of God.

3. **Words are not enough. We carefully choose words with the full knowledge that words are inadequate to express the deepest feelings in our hearts.** In the early nineties a family in our congregation adopted a three-month-old girl. I arranged for the adoption agency to bring the baby to the sanctuary for the presentation of the child to the adoptive parents. As we waited for the coming of the baby, the family joined me in polite conversation, our eyes fixed on the doors

to the sanctuary, our palms were sweating, and our hearts were racing with anticipation. Words are totally inadequate to express what I was feeling when I saw the lady from the adoption agency. She came through the doors and walked down the aisle of the church cradling the beautiful little girl in her arms. It was a holy moment. It was a moment that could not be captured by spoken language. The baby was given to the new parents with grace and beauty. The new father said, "Pastor, pray for us." I could not find the words that I needed so I just prayed, "Thank you." There are times when words are inadequate but we must strive to find the words that make clear what the heart knows.

4. **Public prayer is speech but it is not "mere speech."** It is more than the words that we use; they can mean something or nothing. In spite of the limitations the words of the pastoral prayer laden with compassion, joy, confession, and hope have an almost mystical power to draw us into the presence of Holy. Not easily, not all at once, not every time, but sometimes, the worshipper offers his or her heart without reservation because of the words of the pastoral prayer.

5. **The words of the pastoral prayer are not solitary words.** They are meant for public worship, for the congregation, for all who are assembled to be open to the Spirit. Even those who find it difficult to pray often find an impulse to pray when they are with others. We must never forget that some will pray together who cannot pray alone. It is like two people taking a late evening walk. Each person feels stronger, braver, and more loving because of the near presence of the other. I have found that many who are spiritually weak within themselves can find spiritual strength and awareness of the transcendent when praying with others. Even those who never pray in solitude can experience the Holy Spirit when they are praying with others.

6. **The words that we choose should arise out of the reality of the congregation.** The words should rise from the joys and concerns of the congregants whom we have been called to serve. I know of a pastor who would put a clean index card in his pocket on Monday morning. As the pastor moved through the week he would use his powers of observation and discernment to get in touch with the spiritual and temporal needs of his people and would jot down a note that might or might not be used as he formed the pastoral prayer for the upcoming Sunday. His notes would be about such things as brokenness, loss of hope, dullness of spirit, failure to reflect on God's presence, and all manner of physical and emotional illnesses. Or his notes would be about such things as the joy of new birth, some beam of happiness, some commendable service,

some dawning of new opportunity, some endowment of reason, some power of love, or some knowledge of righteousness. Throughout the week he was pondering about what might be included in the prayer.

7. **The words of the pastoral prayer should also share concern about the community where the church is located.** In all of the congregations that I have attended I have rarely heard a pastor pray, in a specific way, for the town or the immediate neighborhood. The generalities of most of these prayers did not begin to touch the pain or joy of the very people for whom the congregation had a responsibility. I know that the pastor has many concerns in his or her daily life but one does not have to be oblivious to the transcendent things that surface within a few blocks of the church building. The pastor should also muse about world events that bring both hope and harm to all of God's children. The congregation is deeply affected by the events and people that help to shape the reality of the world. They are affected both materially and spiritually by the wind and weather, by the tides and currents and all of the good and evil of the outside world. As the pastoral prayer is prepared the pastor should be keenly aware of those things that are running through the minds and hearts of those who come to worship. These should not be neglected in the pastoral prayer. We should not forget that for some worshippers everything has been eroded, inner forces have evaporated, and there is very little resistance to the power of evil.

Sample Pastoral Prayer

Since I no longer pastor a congregation, my wife and I worship at Brentwood United Methodist Church, which is located near Nashville, Tennessee. The Reverend Kaye Harvey is one of the pastors in this company of believers. The prayers that she offers on Sundays have a way of opening us up to the presence of God. Here is but one example of her well-prepared prayers:

> *Ever-present and Ever-loving God,*
> *We come before you gathering together the cries, concerns, joys, and prayers of all our hearts. Thank you, loving God, that we may pray to You and lay our burdens at the feet of Jesus, who with his compassion carries these burdens with us.*
> *Our prayer is but a response to your ceaseless outpouring of love. When we awake to a new day, you are already there to greet us. When sleepless nights and anxious moments toss us, you are there to comfort us. When difficult choices confuse us, you are there to guide us. You love us before we ever turn to you. You are present in this holy sanctuary with us now, and we are grateful.*

We place before you our lives—fragmented, busy, tired, anxious. We are often in such a hurry that we catch only a glimpse of your beauty and joy. Teach us to slow down, Lord, and not miss a moment of living in your grace.

We place before you our family and friends—forging ministry, caring for the hurt, seeking the lost, striving to be disciples of Christ, clinging to the best of our past while anticipating the hope of the future. Teach us to faithfully walk in the way of your Son, and empower us with your authority to love, care, and proclaim in word and deed the good news of Jesus Christ.

We place before you this world—broken and fighting, yearning for justice and freedom, suffering from drought and greed. Teach us the path of peace, the way of sharing, the brighter vision.

We place before you our gifts, talents, desires, and ambitions, our dreams, for your blessing and for your use in bringing your kingdom on earth as it is in heaven. Use us, Lord, for your higher purpose.

All this we pray in the name of the one who teaches us perfect love, our Lord and Savior Jesus Christ, who taught us this prayer: Our Father . . .

— *Rev. Kaye Harvey*

In conclusion, I want to say that the pastoral prayer should be rooted in the belief that our hearts can be opened to the presence of God and His Christ. The prayer should be offered from the depths of the pastor's soul if there is to be a sure consciousness of God's presence. The hearts of the worshippers will be directed toward the heart of God only when the heart of the pastor is directed toward the heart of God. If we pray from the heart with well-chosen words the living Christ might choose to fill our lives with the power of love, with a sense of the beautiful, and with an understanding of righteousness.

> **The pastoral prayer should be rooted in the belief that our hearts can be opened to the presence of God and His Christ.**

Fifty years ago Harry Emerson Fosdick wrote a book entitled *A Book of Public Prayers*. These were prayers that he had offered while he was pastor of Riverside Church in New York. This book shows the reader how much Fosdick cared about the importance of the pastoral prayer. Here is one example:

Eternal Spirit, grant us grace to worship thee in spirit and in truth. Thou hast so made us that the glory of our lives is not in things below us that we master, but in the Divine above us that masters us. . . . Grant us an hour of such spiritual wealth . . . lifted out of our littleness by dedication to abiding values and to thine everlasting purpose. . . .

Minister to our intimate personal needs. Spirit of the living God, walk through this congregation now and be the help and comfort, the inspiration and sustenance of our souls. In temptation, in illness, in disappointment and depression, in defeat when we are tempted to give up and in success when we are tempted to be proud, O God, restore our souls. May we hear thy voice speaking to each of us, reassuring us, challenging us, summoning us to dedicated and victorious living. . . .

For our nation we pray that it may not miss the true path amid the world's confusion. For all efforts to create an ordered and peaceful human family our petitions rise—for our own sakes, for our children's sakes, and for Christ's sake, that he may see fulfilled the faith and hope for which he died. And for thy Church Universal we pray. Bind up her dissevered fellowship; enlarge her thought, her sense of mission, and the outreach of her service, that she may proclaim and practice the Gospel of thy Son that thy Kingdom may come and thy will be done on earth.

Hear now the unspoken prayers that rise in silence from the deeps of our hearts, and to those needs that can find no voice save for thine ear alone minister according to the riches of thy grace in Christ Jesus, our Lord. Amen. [12]

Ideas to Consider

- A personal prayer life is vital to the leading of pastoral prayers. Recall the story of the wise rabbi and his advice to the questioner.
- Be aware of and involved in the local community. Often, the needs of the community are on the hearts and minds of those in the pews.
- Pennel says, "The hearts of the worshippers will be directed toward the heart of God only when the heart of the pastor is directed toward the heart of God." Have you found this to be true in your own congregation?

F.O.C.U.S.—LIVING A LIFE OF PRAYER*

Tyrone Gordon

Tyrone Gordon *serves as the pastor of St. Luke "Community" United Methodist Church in Dallas, Texas, one of the fastest-growing churches in the United States. Gordon explains how and why a personal prayer life enables pastors to experience revival and rely more fully on God.*

Lord, teach us to pray. —Luke 11:1

It all hit me one morning in the spring of 1992 in Wichita, Kansas. While serving the Saint Mark United Methodist Church, I had given all I had to give but I had drained myself in the process. That alone was part of the problem—I thought I needed to replenish myself. After five years in a fast-growing congregation and being touted as a "successful" pastor, I was running on spiritual fumes.

Sometimes life drives home lessons that we can never forget as well as some things we should never forget. But more important, these hard times can help us grow into focused and committed disciples the Lord is calling for today. Some things will *drive us* to our knees but *being driven to our knees* can be a good thing, because it is there that God will teach us to pray.

Prayer took on a new role in my life, my ministry, and in the church. I had always heard my mentor and predecessor, Dr. Zan Wesley Holmes, Jr., tell us in seminary that we preachers need to be in the Word to hear a word from the Lord *for ourselves* and not just to preach a word *to others*! Preachers need to hear God speak through the Bible, and we should not just open it to find a sermon.

We preachers need to be in the Word to hear a word from the Lord *for ourselves* and not just to preach a word *to others*!

You Can't Give What You Don't Have

During that time of relaxation, reflection, and revival, it became clear that was exactly what I was doing! Here I had been trying to feed others while not allowing God to feed me. I was suffering from spiritual anorexia. Even now, I remember an old gospel song I used to hear the choir sing at the Mount Moriah Baptist Church in Los Angeles: "Fill my cup, fill it up and make me whole!" I needed filling and I needed it fast.

* *This article is an excerpt from* F.O.C.U.S. Living the Lord's Prayer *(Abingdon Press, 2008) and is used by permission from the publisher.*

Something had to be done! A refocus and retooling had to take place! A reexamination of my life, my heart, my faith, and my mind had to happen! I had to get back on track. So I resolved, then and there, that prayer had to be at the center of everything, including my ministry—perhaps even [be] my ministry! Funny that a preacher had to make that decision, but that was where I was in a dark and dramatic time of my life. It was during that time of prayer that God did what God does—God helps us see who we are in relation to God and reminds us that we are not all alone. All of our help comes from the Lord.

Prayer Allows God to Do Something With You

Prayer is *not* rubbing on a magic lamp or bottle and out pops a miracle at our request; but prayer is allowing God to do something *with* me, my life, and my ministry, and the church, God's church! Prayer causes us to look up to God who then is seen and who then becomes the source of our strength for abundant life and ministry.

Prayer is a lifestyle and not just a certain moment in the day or evening. We breathe prayer. We live prayer.

God gave me a new lease on life and ministry through the power of prayer. Developing a personal time of prayer and devotion became a pressing priority; but it also became more. Prayer became a lifestyle, essential to my spiritual survival. The power of prayer began to teach that this is not petty, human business—this is God's business! It is not dependent upon us, but it is dependent upon God. Prayer, then, takes a load off of our shoulders because we now know that we are not carrying this load alone. Jesus bears the yoke; we simply walk beside him obediently. It makes us, as Dr. Zan Holmes would preach, "check our egos at the door!" Once again, the vernacular of the elderly members of the church while I was growing up came to mind and reminded me that, "Prayer is the key to the kingdom and faith unlocks the door." Wow! That experience taught me something about prayer that I had long overlooked. Prayer is a lifestyle and not just a certain moment in the day or evening. We breathe prayer. We live prayer. We move in the power of prayer. We operate through prayer.

Ideas to Consider

- Are you feeding others without allowing God to feed you? Are you suffering from "spiritual anorexia"?
- Consider Gordon's notion that prayer allows God to do something with you if prayer becomes your lifestyle—if you breathe, live, and operate through prayer. How would this make a person more open and usable by God?

BRINGING PRAYER INTO DECISION MAKING AND GOVERNANCE

K. C. Ptomey

K. C. Ptomey *was the senior pastor of Westminster Presbyterian Church for over twenty years. He is now the Louis H. and Katherine S. Zbinden Professor of Pastoral Ministry and Leadership at Austin Presbyterian Theological Seminary in Austin, Texas. In this article, he describes how his congregation practiced using prayer and silence and discusses the mixed responses of church members.*

Prayer is, typically, part of every church meeting or proceeding. Too often these "devotionals" are insipid or trivial or canned; something to rush through in order to get to the real purpose of the gathering: the business.

The leader of one of our committees begins each meeting with an order of evening prayer rather than a canned devotion. Over time this practice became the preferred way to begin our meetings. A staff member, however, took us to a deeper level. In charge of evening prayer that night, she prepared the room by softening the lighting and placing a table with a candle and Bible in the center of the meeting space. She placed signs in the hallway that read, "Enter in silence." At the door of the meeting room was a small waterfall and a candle. Instead of gathering in loud chatter and laugher, members arrived in silence and sat quietly, preparing for the opening worship.

The responses to this new manner of opening meetings were mixed. For some, it was a helpful preparation and much appreciated time for de-stressing and meditating. Others began arriving late, coming only at the time when they knew the business of the meeting would begin. The behavior of these committee members is a microcosm of our culture. It is difficult for many people to appreciate the value of the discipline of silence. The press of business takes precedence over the nurture of our spiritual lives; all the more reason for church leaders to encourage and nurture spiritual practices, including prayer and silence.

Ideas to Consider

- Does the prayer aspect of your church meetings and gatherings feel "trivial or canned"? If so, how could the introduction of meditative silence transform this prayer time?
- How can prayer and silence be incorporated into your congregational routines and practices?

SERVICES OF DAILY PRAISE AND PRAYER

Andy Langford

Andy Langford, *a United Methodist pastor in Western North Carolina, has authored several books focusing on worship and faith and worked extensively on the United Methodist Hymnal. Andy explores how and why the prayer practices of Jesus and his disciples can be modeled in today's congregations. Tracing the patterns of prayer of the church through the centuries, he offers an adaptable daily Praise and Prayer Service.*

Can Christians today learn about prayer from the first followers of Jesus Christ? Jesus' wisdom and strength came from the time he spent with God in prayer. Jesus prayed morning, noon, and night. He prayed when alone by himself; he prayed with other people; he prayed in public; he prayed in the Jerusalem temple; and he prayed even while on the cross. Jesus Christ also encouraged his disciples to pray together regularly.

Following the example of Jesus, the early followers became people of prayer. The first chapter of The Acts of the Apostles observes that the first disciples "were constantly devoting themselves to prayer" (Acts 1:14). Throughout the early centuries, Christians gathered every day to pray.

Even more specifically, from the earliest days of the church, Christians saw the rising of the sun and the lighting of evening lamps as symbolic of Christ's victory over sin and death. With the rising of the sun, Christians celebrated the resurrection of Jesus Christ from the dead. As the sun set and candles were lighted, they remembered that the Word is the true light of the world who will come again in glory. No wonder one of the titles non-Christians used for these passionate pray-ers was those who "invoke" the name of God (Acts 9:14, 21). Praying together gave early Christians their common identity. The prayer services that Christians observed in the first three centuries may be a model for congregations today.

Following the example of Jesus, the early followers became people of prayer. . . . Praying together gave early Christians their common identity.

The earliest Christian prayer services were simple adaptations of Jewish prayer services with distinctive Christological emphases: praise and proclamation of the mystery of the life, death, and resurrection of Jesus Christ followed by prayers of petition and intercession (Philippians 4:6; Colossians 4:2; 1 Thessalonians 5:16-18) and the Lord's Prayer. The services were not long teaching services, but short exclamations of thanksgiving: praise for God's mighty acts in Jesus Christ and the human response of petition. For persecuted people in an oppressive culture, these simple, brief, and focused rites enabled the struggling community to survive.

By the second and third centuries, Christians developed a basic pattern of daily prayer. At the opening and closing of day, Christians gathered in homes to sing particular psalms and biblical songs, offer a series of petitions, and pray together as Jesus had taught his disciples. As the sun rose or as evening candles were lit, they invited God to watch over them throughout the day and protect them through the night. Following the rhythm of nature, the early Christians recognized the enduring presence of Jesus Christ in their midst.

Patterns of Christian prayer during the first three centuries of the church continue to shape contemporary prayer life of every denomination. While drawing upon these earliest traditions, every Christian communion today has developed its own distinctive ways of offering daily prayer. In some traditions there are formal prayers three, six, or nine times a day with particular psalms, readings, and songs. In other informal traditions, a Sunday evening or a mid-week service of praise and testimony is a highlight of the week.

In light of recent liturgical reforms, contemporary Services of Daily Praise and Prayer, based on those of the ancient church, follow a simple structure. Here are some suggestions for adapting one of these services in a local congregation.

Patterns of Christian prayer during the first three centuries of the church continue to shape contemporary prayer life of every denomination. While drawing upon these earliest traditions, every Christian communion today has developed its own distinctive ways of offering daily prayer.

As people gather in a circle, the most important liturgical sign is light and possibly a cross. For Morning Prayer, open the window shades or stand outside to watch the rising sun. For Evening Prayer, observe the sun set or light a candle. Music may or may not be involved, depending on the gifts of the community. Any of these services may be led by a pastor or layperson, possibly rotating the leadership. Some denominational books of prayer and worship have Praise and Prayer services for morning and evening or you may try this flexible pattern using the format from *When You Pray*:

Becoming Aware of God's Presence
For Morning prayer: "O Lord, open our lips and we shall declare your praise."
For Evening Prayer: "Light and peace in Jesus Christ, thanks be to God."
Or read Psalm 141:1-3.

Inviting God's Intervention
Read the Scripture for the week from *When You Pray* or select a verse that asks for God's presence and help.

[optional] **Hymn or Song**
Sing a song appropriate to the time of day or occasion.
For Morning Prayer: "Morning Has Broken" or other song of thanksgiving.
For Evening Prayer: "Dona Nobis Pacem" or a peaceful chorus.
Offer a short blessing for the gift of gathering for prayer.

Listening for God's Voice
Read a brief biblical text. This is not a service for a devotional or short talk but quiet meditation on the Word. The Scripture for the day in *When You Pray* can be used here.

Reflection Time
Allow a few minutes for silent reflection to follow the Scripture.

Making Our Requests Known
Prayer for Our World, Its People and Leaders
Prayer for the Church and Its Leaders
Prayer for Those in Our Circle of Responsibility
Prayer for Ourselves

Offer a series of open petitions, leaving time between each request for silent or spoken prayers. The leader, for example, invites each person to pray first for the world, its people and leaders, and then leaves time for a response before moving to inviting prayer for the church and its leaders. Imagine a series of concentric circles gradually widening until all creation has been included. Everyone may respond to each prayer with "Lord, hear our prayer," or a short song such as the Taizé "Jesus, Remember Me." The prayer may end with an invitation for all the saints, faithful persons who now worship Christ face-to-face, to join in the prayer. Another option is simply to invite everyone to pray extemporaneously.

Offering of Self to God
Close with an offering of ourselves to God. You might use the week's Offering of Self to God from *When You Pray*, such as these lines from Wesley's Covenant Service used in Week 4:
"Let me be your servant, under your command.
I will no longer be my own.
I will give up myself to your will in all things." [13]

Blessing
End with a short blessing.
For Morning Prayer: "May the love of Jesus Christ surround you this day."
For Evening Prayer: "May Jesus Christ enfold you this night."

Such daily Services of Praise and Prayer have many possibilities in local congregations. While the whole congregation gathers on Sundays for a full Service of the Word and Holy Communion, these prayer services are a daily remembrance of Christ's eternal presence by smaller, pre-existing groups in the church. If every group in every congregation prayed at each gathering, they move their whole community toward ceaseless prayer.

Morning Prayer may be celebrated by the staff of a congregation before the workday begins, at the start of a women's group, at the beginning of a Sunday school class, or at a men's breakfast. Evening Prayer may be offered at the close of a youth meeting, committee session, or a workday. When a church goes on a mission trip, participates in a spiritual retreat, builds a Habitat for Humanity house, or gathers for a church dinner, instead of offering a brief prayer alone, expand the horizon of the congregation and help them unite with the church throughout the ages through a Service of Praise and Prayer. How may your congregation develop its own rhythm of Services of Praise and Prayer?

Ideas to Consider

- Andy notes several emphases of prayer services throughout the centuries, both formal and informal traditions. What key elements appeal to your congregation/community?
- Are there regular gatherings within your congregation that could adopt a Service of Praise and Prayer? Perhaps you could start with a retreat or weekly Bible study group.

F.O.C.U.S.—God Will Equip You With Power*

Tyrone Gordon

Tyrone Gordon *serves as he pastor of St. Luke "Community" United Methodist Church in Dallas, Texas, one of the fastest-growing churches in the United States. Gordon talks about prayer as a way of living the gospel of Jesus Christ. Prayer, Gordon says, nables us see to the power of God at work and empowers us to do what God wants.*

Our ministries should be the product of prayer. Our lives should be a reflection of prayer! The importance of prayer, fasting, Scripture reading, and other spiritual disciplines once again became a part of my spiritual diet. They had to, if I wanted to continue to grow as a spiritual leader of God's people. So often we preachers, pastors, and spiritual leaders try to go it alone and do it by ourselves. But we cannot do God's business without God's power! God's power is unleashed through us and works through us only as we are connected to our spiritual source, which comes through prayer, the Word, worship, and the practice of the spiritual disciplines. Prayer brought me back! Prayer refocused me! Prayer centered me!

I began to reorganize every ministry around prayer, and it began a journey that teaches the very aspects of prayer in the life of the spiritual leader, the leadership, and the congregation and its ministries. How can we stay in a perpetual state of communion with the holy and go about our everyday routine, ministries, and lives? What does it mean to always pray or pray without ceasing? Then it hit me, prayer is not something we do—prayer is who we are! There might be designated times of prayer but it must go further than that. Prayer shapes our lives and penetrates our thought process; it informs our decisions, influences our conduct, and inspires our actions.

Prayer is not designed to get God to do what we want; rather, prayer empowers us to do what God wants. Prayer is the connection be-

We cannot do God's business without God's power! God's power is unleashed through us and works through us only as we are connected to our spiritual source.

tween ourselves and the holy so that God can move *us* in ways that we did not know we could be moved. God empowers us to do things we once thought were impossible to accomplish! Through prayer, we not only see God at work in the world; we allow God to be at work in us!

---

* *This article is an excerpt from* F.O.C.U.S. Living the Lord's Prayer *(Abingdon Press, 2008) and is used by permission from the publisher.*

Prayer is a lifestyle inspired, informed, and directed by the Holy Spirit to do God's will upon this Earth through us and with us. Prayer moves the church and its ministries to be in line with God's purposes for that particular place. When prayer becomes the lifestyle of individuals and the church rather than simply a set-aside time or a particular ministry that tells God everything God already knows, we then learn to pray without ceasing. Our lives become our time of prayer. We begin to see God's power unleashed in the congregation and in the life of the pastor and leadership. Through prayer we become *focused* on our mission, clear in our vision, and undying to our commitment to the gospel of Jesus Christ. When a church's very foundation for ministry is prayer, a new spirit takes shape. The church births new life and a new sense of optimism—even more, a strong faith takes hold! A church that bathes all it does in prayer is an exciting church. It is a church that can't wait to see what God's about to do next in its midst. A praying church is a church that does not depend on itself, its name, or its buildings and budgets to get ministry done; rather, it depends on the power of God that is at work among the people who are busy doing what God has called the church to do.

Prayer is not something we do—prayer is who we are!

There is power when God's people live prayer and not just say their prayers. Therefore, we are invited by Christ to grow into a life of prayer.

Ideas to Consider

- Gordon says, "Our ministries should be the product of prayer." When prayer precedes action, the outcome is alignment with God's purpose.
- How do we pray without ceasing? Gordon says we must make prayer a lifestyle—allow prayer to penetrate our thought process, inform our decisions, influence our conduct, and inspire our actions.

CALL TO PRAYER

Marilyn E. Thornton

Marilyn E. Thornton is a minister, musician, story-teller, and educator who loves to tell the story of God's salvation for all people, using different media. She is pastor of Emery United Methodist Church in Murfreesboro, Tennessee, and the lead editor of African American resources at Abingdon Press. In this article, Thornton describes her experience of prayer in South Africa and how the daily calls to prayer from the surrounding mosques were a nudging reminder to pause and pray.

In 2000, I went to South Africa with a group, intent on studying the Truth and Reconciliation process. What we got was a study on intentional prayer. In Johannesburg (Jo'burg), we stayed at a Catholic retreat center run by white nuns. Guests included black priests from neighboring countries. In Cape Town, we stayed at an Anglican retreat center that was owned by the oldest Coloured Anglican church in town. Both centers were located close to mosques; in Jo'burg, one large mosque, and in Cape Town, several, all of which issued the call to prayer five times a day, bringing new meaning to:

Make a joyful noise to the LORD, all the earth.
  Worship the LORD with gladness;
    come into his presence with singing.
                    — Psalm 100:1-2

It also brought a new consciousness to what it means to pray without ceasing.

South Africa has a significant Muslim population (as do most African nations). However, some of these Muslims are descendants of Malaysians (now considered Coloureds) whose ancestors were brought to South Africa as slaves by the Dutch as early as 1657. The newly arriving Europeans had first attempted to enslave the native population of Khoi-khoi-san (Bushmen). But like the Native Americans in the evolving United States, the Khoi-khoi-san proved ill-suited to farming and ranching operations based on an ideology of land and human ownership. After working for a time, their knowledge of the land would allow them to merely disappear into the landscape, taking the cattle with them. As the English turned to Black Africa to work the lands of America, the Dutch turned to Madagascar and Asia to work the land in South Africa, to people who already had a Muslim background. Additionally, the Dutch, who also occupied the East Indies, would exile the Muslim leaders of the resistance there, to Cape Town. These imams used their imprisonment to teach other prisoners and slaves a faith that required prayer to God five times a day.

Prayer is one of the five pillars of Islam. Wherever they are, at the appointed times, you will find Muslim males unrolling their prayer mats, and kneeling down to pray. In the towns and villages, five times a day, the imams lift their voices to issue a call to prayer. In large cities like Jo'burg and Cape Town, the call is chanted over a loudspeaker. In Cape Town, when the various imams extended the call to prayer one within moments of the other, their voices would create several lines of the same melody, indeed a joyful noise and a polyphonic pull on the soul, arresting my thoughts and requiring my spirit to join the people in prayer. And while the call reminded the faithful Muslim males to put down their tools and come to the mosque, I noticed that others at the Christian retreat centers where we stayed, upon hearing the invitation to worship, also stopped what they were doing and entered into the presence of God through prayer. More than being an obligation to honor God, prayer is a time and space to be in communication with God, to remember that we live and move and have our being in God (Acts 17:28), who invites us to live in community by keeping God at the center of our lives.

More than being an obligation to honor God, prayer is a time and space to be in communication with God.

The Islamic call to prayer is a sung affirmation that outlines the basic Muslim understanding of God:

God is most great. God is most great.
God is most great. God is most great.
I testify that there is no God except God.
I testify that there is no God except God.
I testify that Muhammad is the messenger of God.
I testify that Muhammad is the messenger of God.
Come to prayer! Come to prayer!
Come to success! Come to success!
God is most great. God is most great.
There is none worthy of worship except God.

The call invites the people to come. Come where success can be found. There is no better place to discover greatness than in the life of God.

In Jo'burg and Cape Town, as the call to prayer tugged on my heart, I would sometimes bow my head and murmur the prayer that Jesus taught his disciples:

Our Father, who art in heaven,
    hallowed be thy name.
    Thy kingdom come,
    thy will be done on earth as it is in heaven.

With this prayer, I addressed God as the universal parent, our daddy, who loves all the children, whether Christian or Muslim, Black, White, or Coloured, whether descendants of slaves or descendants of slaveholders, whether promoters of freedom or promoters of oppression; all are sinners to whom grace has been extended. The Lord's Prayer is one that acknowledges the sovereignty of God over the entire universe, over all the people and all of creation. It speaks to the holiness of the name of God and the desire that God's kingdom come in its fullness; that God's will be accomplished in completeness, throughout the entire world, everywhere we go. By praying the prayer of my Jewish Savior, the Lord Jesus Christ, I, too, affirmed that there is no greatness and no success outside of life in God as we move toward a condition of *shalom*, where there is no failure, no oppression, no poverty, no apartheid, no racism, and no divisions, where all can see others as God sees them, as children of the Most High God.

> **By praying the prayer of my Jewish Savior, the Lord Jesus Christ, I, too, affirmed that there is no greatness and no success outside of life in God.**

As I stood on the ground of the continent from which my ancestors were stolen, I would sometimes respond to the chanted call to prayer by breaking out in song, coming into the presence of God with singing. These songs of faith enabled me to pray without ceasing in the patois of my forebears in places where Latin, Afrikaans, Zulu, Swahili, Xhosa, English, and Arabic may have been the language of choice. I prayed to God who is everywhere I go and who hears and answers prayer in every language, should we only respond to the call.

Ideas to Consider

- For Marilyn, the Islamic call to prayer served as a reminder of the importance of the practice of prayer. She welcomed this constant call as a reminder to thoughtfully enter into God's presence.
- Marilyn says she often sings prayers to God. This frequent and personal prayer practice enables Thornton to, in essence, pray without ceasing.

A PATTERN FOR PERSONAL PRAYER RETREAT

Rueben P. Job

Rueben P. Job, *a retired* **United Methodist bishop,** *was formerly World Editor of The Upper Room publishing program. His previous publications include* **Three Simple Rules, A Wesleyan Spiritual Reader,** *and* **A Guide to Retreat for All God's Shepherds,** *from which this article has been excerpted.***

This excerpt from *A Guide to Retreat for All God's Shepherds* is designed to assist you and your congregation in a time of reflection, prayer, and renewal. The *Guide* is presented with the deep awareness that God is the leader of every spiritual retreat and is the guide of our life's journey. You join a multitude of persons who have discovered that a time of retreat is often the setting in which God brings new strength, new clarity, courage, and direction to life's journey.

Preparation for personal retreat will include selection of the place and time. Often space can be found in a church, retreat center, house of prayer, or even a park. However, if it is not possible to use a place other than your own home or office, do not let that prevent you from being in God's presence and listening to God's call. If you use your own home, select a place that will permit silence and solitude. The most important thing is that you "come apart" from the distractions of your daily routine in order to hear more clearly and be more attentive to the gentle voice of the One who seeks to be your guide.

Preparations should include meals (unless you are fasting—then adequate fluids), a place to rest, and allow some exercise opportunities. You will bring your Bible and you may wish to bring a second translation to enrich your Scripture reading. Also, bring a notebook and pen. Upon starting your retreat, get settled and consciously withdraw to this time of intimate interaction with God.

The water for which we thirst is God's grace, but God gives us the job of hauling it with our own buckets![14]

Patterns are meant to be a guide. In some instances they are to be followed without variation and in others, variation gives the pattern character and individuality. Listen carefully to God's voice within this retreat and be sensitive to how God may guide you to adjust the patterns to suit your needs. I encourage you to use this pattern two or three times to see whether it can become a model in your own

---

* *This article is an excerpt from* A Guide to Retreat for All God's Shepherds *(Abingdon Press, 1994) and is used by permission from the publisher.*

spiritual journey. The points of tension you feel may be the points of growth. However, after several retreats, you may be ready to modify the pattern to lead you more effectively toward God.

— Prayer for Guidance

The prayer for guidance can reflect your movement toward God and your invitation for God's intervention in your life. This can be a time of centering your thoughts and offering this time of retreat and yourself to the One from whom you anticipate guidance and direction and with whom you seek communion. Spend time with a printed prayer or one that you write. Move on only after you have placed as much of yourself and this time apart as you can into God's care and under God's direction.

— Silent Listening

With a note pad near, spend time in quiet listening for the voice of the One "who has nothing to learn from you but everything to tell you." Do not be distracted by the many images, ideas, and feelings that flood your silence. Simply call yourself back to attentiveness to God with a brief prayer or invitation, such as, "Come, Holy Spirit," or offering, "Here I am, Lord," and continue the silent listening.

— Scripture Reading

Read your selected Scripture passage several times. Try to let the passage address you with its questions and affirmations. "What is God saying to me in this passage?" Permit the passage to be God's message for you at this particular time and place. Note your feelings, questions, affirmations, and direction that come into your awareness. Plan to allow at least one uninterrupted hour for this part of your retreat.

— Spiritual Reading

Read from other inspirational writings you may have chosen to bring with you. Read to hear the voice of God rather than to get information or to seek ideas. Ask what God is saying to you through the particular text today. Allow at least one hour for this time of listening to the saints. Read slowly and reflectively, pausing for words, phrases, or ideas that capture your attention.

— Reflection

Gather the notes taken during your time of silent listening, Scripture reading, and spiritual reading. Read them and note and record any common themes or messages. Allow at least one hour for reflection. Return to your notes or the readings as often as it is helpful. Record your reflections.

— Mealtime

Receiving food with a thankful heart can be a helpful reminder of the many ways we are sustained by the abundance of God's grace. If you entered your retreat in the midst of a fast, you may wish to end your fast with a meal of thanksgiving during or at the end of your retreat. You will discover mealtimes to be a feast that goes far beyond food.

— Rest

People often come to a retreat in great need of rest. If this is true for you, feel no embarrassment about resting. An hour or two of rest or sleep may be the most important part of your retreat. However, if you feel a longer time is needed, or if you are consistently exhausted, consult your physician and visit with a trusted spiritual guide.

— Recreation

Follow a rest period with exercise. If possible, go outdoors to walk, jog, swim, garden, chop wood, or rake leaves. Of course, exercise within your capacity and at a level appropriate to your physical condition. If your physical activity is restricted, an hour outdoors, even with modest activity, can be a refreshing and rewarding part of your retreat.

— Journaling

Record in your journal what has been happening during this retreat. Note any questions and directions that have surfaced as well as the affirmations you have experienced and any commitments you wish to make.

— Prayer

Offer your own prayers of adoration, thanksgiving, petition, intercession, and abandonment into God's care. Allow time for God to lead you in prayer with the knowledge that even when we do not know how to pray as we ought or desire, the Spirit intercedes and leads us in our life of prayer (Romans 8:26).

— Further Spiritual Reading, Reflection, and Journaling

If you have time or wish to extend your retreat, continue the process of spiritual reading, reflection, journaling, and reading the Scriptures and other resources you have brought with you.

— Eucharist

Many find the celebration of the Eucharist to be a singularly formative and renewing experience while on retreat. Use the appropriate liturgy for the seasons or one that you have found to be particularly helpful and formative.

— Response

This is the time to focus, gather, and record your response to all that has been happening to you. This may include a wide range of things from a simple prayer of thanksgiving to writing a new rule or way of life for yourself, or renewing commitments and covenants in past times.

— Returning to the World

Many times we return from a retreat renewed and ready only to discover that our renewed insight, vision, and spiritual energy quickly drain away. Consider and record the steps you intend to take to permit God to continue leading you toward maturity in Christ.

— Closing Prayer

This will be a time of thanksgiving, petition, and commitment as you prepare to return to the demands and opportunities of your life. You may wish to use a printed prayer or your own personal prayer.

Ideas to Consider

- Rueben says that "a time of retreat is often the setting in which God brings new strength, new clarity, courage, and direction to life's journey." Does this encourage you to plan a personal retreat or a time of retreat with your leadership team? When will you go?
- Consider texts such as Rueben's *Guide to Retreat* or *When You Pray* when you plan a personal retreat. These can be helpful guides for contemplation, prayer, and renewal.

FREQUENTLY ASKED QUESTIONS ABOUT PRAYER

Does God hear me?
Does it make a difference when I pray?
Can prayers heal?

When prayer is taken seriously, concerns and questions will emerge. Leaders will have explored many of these questions themselves but must guard against the temptation to dismiss or take lightly the questions that arise from others as they begin a deepening life of prayer.

Your personal preparation will include reviewing with your leadership team some of what others have said about prayer and then confirming your own response to the easy and the difficult questions.

The mystery of prayer ensures that there are no simple answers. No one set of responses will be right for each community or each person. It's an ongoing conversation and an unending journey.

Whether your leadership team is two or three people who meet with you or a staff of twenty, you can feel confident and ready to engage the questions you will receive. What can you do together to prepare to fully model, encourage, and lead in prayer? (These opening suggestions have already been presented as part of a year-long approach to prayer on pages 7–16.)

1. First, begin a personal prayer practice. Pray alone and together. Time for personal prayer every day will not only renew your spirit but give you experiences to share, tools to talk about, and a fresh and relevant point of view. As a team, follow together *When You Pray*. The Scripture and themes are tied to the lectionary but can be used by all. Praying together is an essential way to begin.

2. Find a time for a prayer retreat with a small group of leaders in your congregation. Whether you can take several days, an overnight, or even just a day at a nearby park, set aside a time away from the busy responsibilities of daily life for prayer and introspection together. (You'll find a useful guide to retreat on page 50.)

3. Read about prayer and spiritual practices, whether you read new books or old favorites. Experience the language and the conversation about prayer. Read authors you love, authors who make you think, and some with whom you disagree. Flex your muscles. Several good choices could include *Prayer: Does It Make Any Difference?* by Philip Yancey; *Dimensions of Prayer* by Douglas Steere; *Prayer: Finding the Heart's True Home* by Richard Foster;

> **O begin! Fix some part of every day for private exercises. . . . Do justice to your own soul; give it time and means to grow. Do not starve yourself any longer.**[15]
> — *John Wesley*

Open Mind, Open Heart by Thomas Keating; *Leading a Life With God* by Daniel Wolpert; or *The Workbook of Living Prayer* by Maxie Dunnam.

4. As a team of leaders or a group of friends and colleagues, talk through the tough questions of prayer. Together come up with responses and practice them together. Go deep and question each other. Argue. Can you talk about prayer with hope and confidence?

5. As you gain a renewed confidence and vocabulary about the practice of prayer, test your comfort with uncertainty. At its heart, communication with God is a great and gracious mystery. Talk together about where you feel a sense of certainty and where you accept lack of certainty. Where does the mystery bring you comfort and where does it cause you dis-ease?

Whether you agree or disagree, writers can often help others begin to find clearer expression. In the pages following, you'll find a few excerpts from writers well known for effective writing on prayer. As you read these writers and other books and articles on prayer, look for answers and guidance in how you'll answer the hard questions.

What's the purpose of prayer?
Does God hear me?
Does it make a difference when I pray?
Do prayers help with healing?
I prayed but nothing happened. Was I lacking in my faith?
Can I change God's mind with my prayers?
I want to pray, but I don't know what to say or ask for.
Does God know the details of my life and circumstance?
God does not answer when I pray.

Receiving Answers to Prayer

In his book, *Prayer: Does It Make Any Difference?*, Philip Yancey says:

Prayer that is based on relationship and not transaction may be the most freedom-enhancing way of connecting to a God whose vantage point we can never achieve and can hardly imagine.[16]

What Can I Pray For?

Philip Yancey quotes his friend the Rev. David Mains and the checklist he recommends to be sure that prayers are on target:

1. *What do I really want?* Am I being specific, or am I just rambling about nothing in particular?
2. *Can God grant this request?* Or is it against God's nature to do so?
3. *Have I done my part?* Or am I praying to lose weight when I haven't dieted?
4. *How is my relationship with God?* Are we on speaking terms?
5. *Who will get the credit if my request is granted?* Do I have God's interests in mind?
6. *Do I really want my prayer answered?* What would happen if I actually did get that girlfriend back?[17]

What Does It Mean to Pray for Others?

Maxie Dunnam, in his book *The Workbook of Living Prayer*,[18] discusses the topic of intercessory prayer:

It is the testimony of people who practice living prayer that things happen when we pray that do not happen when we don't pray. People are healed, situations change, conditions are altered, persons find direction, revivals come, even the courses of nations are redirectered.

It appears that God has so ordered life and the world that our praying is a vital part of the redemptive plan for individuals and the entire universe. Through intercessory prayer God does something that would not otherwise be done. There are numerous facets to intercessory prayer, some that we have experienced, no doubt many that are yet undiscovered. There is one dimension that is such a part of life that we need to give it attention now in our adventure in living prayer. Intercessory prayer is a ministry of love and care.

Consider the possibilities for such a ministry.
1. Intercession is an identification of love. Clarence Jordan, in his *Cotton Patch Gospel* version of the New Testament, translates that signal word

in 2 Cor. 5:19: "In Christ God was reconciling the world to himself . . ." in this fashion: "God was in Christ, hugging the world to Himself."

That's what we do when we pray. We put our arms around another person, a relationship, a situation, our community—even the world—and hug it to ourselves and to God in love. In a mysterious way that we may never understand, something always happens to us, and sometimes in those for whom we pray.

2. Intercessory prayer opens our minds to hear what else God wants to tell us about the way we can minister to others. When we pray for another person, we are centered on that person as well as on God. God can then speak to us about the needs of that other person and how we may be instruments of meeting that need.

3. Intercessory prayer becomes the "launching pad" for our service to others. People often say, "Prayer *alone* is not enough." Frank Laubach, the great practitioner of intercession, reminds us that "prayer that seeks to do God's will is not alone. It will be accompanied by any other approach that God may suggest. It will be accompanied by service, by considerations, by kindnesses of every kind."

4. Intercessory prayer becomes the "power base" for our relationships with others. In my ministry I find that when I pray for persons with whom I am counseling immediately before I see them, the counseling experience is far more effective than when I don't. There was a period in my life when I did not take intercessory prayer seriously. During that time I always felt somewhat frantic and hassled—almost always under pressure for the next appointment or too intense in my relationship with the person with whom I was sharing. Then I began to practice intercessory prayer, always reserving time between appointments to pray for the person with whom I would be counseling. It was revolutionary for me. I was more relaxed in my relationships, sharper in my perception, focused in my attention—but more, something happened in the persons for whom I prayed. They were more relaxed, more open and honest in their sharing, more receptive to me and what I had to offer, willing to accept my inability and often unwillingness to give advice.

Intercessory prayer was the "power base" for my relationships with them. This can be transferred into every area of life. We are empowered to serve others, and we serve with the greatest insight and effectiveness when we pray for those we seek to serve.

5. Intercessory prayer is the investment of ourselves in God's design for God's kingdom among people and nations. Frank Laubach called for a

"prayer army" of ten million people who "would start praying until our minds were in perfect harmony with the will of God . . . who would tip the balance and save the world." He called this a "war of amazing kindness." We have yet to see what could happen should such an army arise!

When Bad Things Happen . . .

Philip Yancey in *Prayer: Does It Make Any Difference?*:

In prayer I ask for, and gradually gain, trust in God's love and justice and mercy and holiness, despite all that might call those traits into question. I immerse myself in the changeless qualities of God and then return to do my part in acting out those qualities on earth: "Your will be done on earth as it is in heaven."[19]

When I Feel Hopeless . . .

Rueben P. Job in *When You Pray: Daily Practices for Prayerful Living*:

It is hope that is the promise of earthshaking and life-changing magnitude. You and I are children of God who are promised our full inheritance as God's beloved. Why should we fear? The living God has promised to be our companion in every experience of life, in this world and the next. No one can separate us from God or from our inheritance as a child of God. It is ours and by God's grace we may claim it now. Paul put it this way, "I pray that the God of our Lord Jesus Christ, the Father of glory, may give you a spirit of wisdom and revelation as you come to know him, so that, with the eyes of your heart enlightened, you may know what is the hope to which he has called you, what are the riches of his glorious inheritance among the saints . . . " (Ephesians 1:17-18).

Hope for wild, wonderful, and too-good-to-be-true results like actual signs of God's kingdom sprouting up all over the world, in your community, and even in your life. And then let your life and your prayer reflect that hope this day and always. Your kingdom come on *earth* as it is in *heaven*. May it be so today![20]

How Do We Pray?

Rueben P. Job in *When You Pray: Daily Practices for Prayerful Living*:

When the disciples asked Jesus to teach them how to pray he taught them the prayer that has been our pattern of prayer ever since. In the Lord's

Prayer, Jesus instructed them in prayer, but he did far more than teach the disciples how to pray, he taught them how to live. In Luke's record Jesus reminds the disciples to stay focused, not on their need or on themselves, but on God. Our culture tells us in a thousand ways to stay focused on ourselves and outdo one another by caring for ourselves first. Jesus tells us that the best way to live fully and faithfully is to outdo one another in loving God and neighbor. To follow Jesus is to choose for ourselves the best way to live.[21]

Does Prayer Work?

Andy Langford, a United Methodist pastor, published author, and writer of various articles in this book, addresses this question:

Sometimes our prayers do not seem effective. Prayer is not magic. Prayer is not like an Aladdin's lamp that, when rubbed with the magic words, produces a genie to grant our wishes. All of us have prayed for something, and our prayers seem unanswered.

Sometimes, the fault is our own by asking for the wrong thing. Like a child at Christmas, if a child asks Santa Claus for a bike and a pony and a swimming pool and a new brother, the requests may not be fully answered. God's answer to our prayers may be "Yes" or "No" or "Not now" or simply silence. Sometimes, we are so busy talking in prayer that we forget to listen. We need to listen as well as speak; to hear as well as to be heard.

Prayer also demands much of us. When we pray, we cannot put all the burden on God to fulfill our prayers. Sometimes effective prayers demand that we behave differently.

What is the value of prayer, therefore, if we are not always certain of the results and if we may have to do lots of the work? Above all, prayer brings us into a stronger relationship with Jesus. The greatest gift we receive in prayer is the gift of the presence of God. Prayer teaches us that we are not alone. Some people describe their experience in prayer as being covered with warm oil, or filled with a warm spirit, or even being hit by an electric bolt. Many of us never have such experiences. But by simply having a close, intimate conversation with God, we learn more about Jesus and more about ourselves. Prayer is most effective when it helps us discern Jesus' presence in our lives; it changes our own personal perspective into God's perspective.

Prayer is most effective when it helps us discern Jesus' presence in our lives; it changes our own personal perspective into God's perspective.

Offering prayers enable us not to bombard God with requests but to bring our desires within the scope of God's compassion. Instead of trying to tip the balance in favor of our loved ones, let us envision that the entire scale and all the weights are in God's hands.

Jesus told us that even if we do not see and hear God in our prayers, God is with us. Jesus said, "Ask, and it will be given you; search, and you will find; knock, and the door will be opened for you. For everyone who asks receives, and everyone who searches finds, and for everyone who knocks, the door will be opened." Jesus then provided an example to prove we can trust God when you pray: "Is there anyone among you who, if your child asks for bread, will give a stone?" Just as we human beings would never give our children anything that would harm them, likewise Jesus declared that God is even more attentive and giving: If you then . . . know how to give good gifts to your children, how much more will your Father in heaven give good things to those who ask him!" (Matthew 7:7-9, 11).

QUESTIONS KIDS HAVE ABOUT PRAYER

Kel Groseclose

Kel Groseclose *is Minister of Congregational Care at First United Methodist Church in Wenatchee, Washington, and is the author of several books, including* Why Did God Make Bugs and Other Icky Things? *(Dimensions for Living, 1992) and* A Moment With God for Grandparents *(Dimensions for Living, 1999).*

Asking questions is a fundamental human right, a gift from God to be highly prized and used whenever needed. God hears our questions the first time we ask and patiently works with us to provide satisfying answers. Some of the most profound questions may take a lifetime to answer; others may have to wait until we're part of eternal life. Just knowing we can ask God any question is comforting both to youngsters and adults. Whether we ask with composure, frustration, or even anger, God always listens.

Children are deeply spiritual and capable of dealing with profound matters. Like adults, they can ask very difficult questions about prayer. I'm certain our Creator appreciates the honest, refreshing prayers of children. They usually tell it like it is and go straight to the heart of the matter. They also pray expecting answers and seldom mince words or try to "butter up" the Almighty. We adults would do well to incorporate that same openness and honesty in our prayer lives.

When visiting with children, I've discovered their prayers are remarkably unselfish. A four-year-old granddaughter of ours said she prayed that her grandparents would **The goal for every follower of Christ is for prayer to become a natural, honest visit with God—perhaps with less talking and more listening.** "stay a little longer so they could see her as a grown-up." When our six-year-old autistic grandson was asked if he prayed, he clasped his hands in front of him and nodded "yes." He indicated he prayed about love ("wawa"), singing ("lala"), and for his grandparents. He was less emphatic about praying for his parents, which seemed to amuse him.

The goal for every follower of Christ is for prayer to become a natural, honest visit with God—perhaps with less talking and more listening. The following questions are not designed to provide quick answers to children's complex questions, but to offer pastors, directors of Christian education, Sunday school teachers, and parents a few helpful insights to consider when formulating age-appropriate responses. These are beginning points for ongoing discussions between experienced and beginning followers of Christ—dialogues where all parties have opportunities to grow spiritually.

The hearts of youngsters are usually tender and receptive to spiritual matters, including prayer. It's vital we offer them solid, insightful, and age-appropriate theological answers, doing so always in caring and affirming ways.

QUESTION #1: How can I know God hears me when I pray?

First, know that God loves you very much and knows you by name. God hears your prayers. Sometimes it may not seem like you get an answer because it may not be what you expect. Grown-ups feel that way too. A big part of prayer is listening for God and what God may be saying to you.

More for older children: You may feel more in tune with God when you pray if you look at the examples in the Bible such as Philippians 4:6 (pray with thanksgiving); James 5:16 (pray for one another); and Romans 8:26 (when we do not know how to pray, God's Spirit intercedes for us). Jesus described prayers that are simple, sincere, and selfless. When you pray this way, you start feeling closer to God from the beginning.

QUESTION #2: If God knows everything about me, why do I need to pray?

God knows everything, so the purpose of prayer is not to tell God what God doesn't know. The purpose of prayer is to be friends with God. When you're best friends with someone, you spend time together, share secrets, laugh and cry together, and just have fun together. God wants this kind of relationship with you! Prayer is simply talking with God and sharing every part of your life with God. The more you pray, the better you will know God and the closer you will feel to God.

More for older children: God knows exactly who you are and loves you just the way you are. But God also wants you to grow in wisdom and faith and become the very best person you can be. God has high hopes for you! As you get older, you will pray about much more than yourself and the things you need or want to happen. You will begin to pray more and more about others and the needs of the world. God wants our prayers and our love for others and for the world to grow as we grow.

QUESTION #3: How can God possibly hear everyone's prayers and not get mine mixed up with somebody else's?

God is very different than we are. Our bodies can be in only one place at a time, and sometimes we have trouble listening to more than one person. But

God is not like us. God is Spirit, and God can do things we cannot even imagine are possible. God loves each and every one of us very much and listens to every word we say or think in prayer.

More for older children: Our Heavenly Parent wants to be involved in every aspect of your life. If God can count every hair on your head (Matthew 10:30), then surely God can keep track of every word you've ever spoken and every thought you've ever had. Remember that you are a child of God, a one-of-a-kind, unrepeatable miracle.

QUESTION #4: Do I always have to fold my hands, shut my eyes, or kneel beside my bed when I pray?

Certainly not! Sometimes shutting your eyes or kneeling can help you to shut out the things that are going on around you and focus on God. The important thing when you pray is not what you do with your body but what you do with your thoughts. God wants all of your attention when you talk to God in prayer—just like a friend wants your attention when you are talking together. That's why it's better not to turn on the TV or do other things when you pray.

More for older children: Of course, you can pray anywhere, anytime. God will hear and answer your prayers, even when you're at a ballgame or a loud concert with thousands of people. But God loves spending quiet moments with you, too. Try to make time for prayer in your busy life. When you do, you will be blessed by your time with God!

QUESTION #5: Will God still love me if I share my mistakes and the bad thoughts I sometimes have?

Yes! We all make mistakes and sometimes have bad thoughts. God wants us to share those things in prayer and ask for forgiveness and help. God always understands, forgives us, and gives us the help we need. It's normal to feel bad or sad or alone sometimes, but God always loves us and wants us to help us through these times.

More for older children: We read about people in the Bible who were frightened and confused. Sometimes they yelled, argued, and even shook their fists toward God in heaven. God understood, forgave them, and even used them to do God's work in the world. Each of us also has times of confusion and doubt—times when we feel separated from God and others. But God's love is always available just for the asking! Remember that God will comfort you and see you through every tough time.

QUESTION #6: Can I help God to answer other people's prayers?

Yes! This is one of the ways God works in the world. God uses people to love and help other people. If you feel God wants you to do something for someone, God will be with you and help you to do it—whether it is being kind to someone who needs a friend, helping someone with some work that needs to be done, giving a hug or a smile to someone who is sad or lonely, or something else. God will show you the needs of others and then give you ideas about how you can help.

More for older children: God uses anyone who is willing to serve, teach, comfort, or pray for others. If you are willing to help, God will give you something to do! And God will prepare you and give you everything you need to succeed in the task. If you still are a little unsure about helping, remember that God understands this and has promised to go with you every step of the way. All you have to do is listen, be courageous, and then "go for it," trusting God to guide you.

**QUESTION # 7: Why is it so hard to pray in front
of others? Will I ever be able to do it?**

It's normal to be nervous when speaking or praying in front of other people. Many grown-ups still find it hard to do. But it's sort of like learning to ride a bike. The more you try it, the easier it gets. If you are nervous, say a silent prayer, asking for God's help. Then keep it short and simple. God doesn't care about fancy or perfect words but about what is in your heart. Your prayer will be beautiful to God!

More for older children: Even the best students, teachers, and pastors sometimes get nervous when asked to pray in a group. In some ways, that may be a good thing, because it shows that they are humble and recognize the importance of prayer. When you feel anxious about praying in front of others, say a quick, silent prayer for God's help and then keep your words honest, heartfelt, and to the point. God will take your humble prayer and use it to speak to the needs of those who are listening.

QUESTION #8: How do I know if God is answering my prayers?

You know God is answering your prayers by the things that happen after you pray. When you have the things you need, when you stop being angry or sad or lonely, when you see others change for the better, when you forgive and are forgiven—these are all signs of answered prayer. If you don't see an answer to prayer right away, that does not mean that God is not working to answer your prayer. Some answers come quickly, and others can take a very long time. Sometimes you have to wait, and sometimes the answer is no. Just like a loving parent sometimes says no, God knows what is best for you and is always working for your good.

More for older children: Signs of answered prayer are all around you, but you have to look for them. When people you've been praying for show signs of spiritual growth, when you see broken relationships healed, when your faith and the faith of those around you becomes deeper, when you grow in compassion and concern for others—those are sure indications that God is working. Try not to become discouraged when prayers seem to go unanswered. Remember that that God has good plans for you and is always working on your behalf. Waiting on answers to prayer can draw you even closer to God, and that is always a good thing.

QUESTION #9: Is it OK to ask God for favors and things?

God knows you have needs and wants, and God wants you to pray about these things because they are important to you. But God also wants you to give thanks for the many gifts God gives you every day. It's also important to tell God how much you love God. Just like a family member or close friend likes to hear you say, "I love you," so does God! Every time you share your thanks and your affection for God, your love for God will grow and your relationship with God will become stronger.

More for older children: Many adults continue to struggle with this question. We live in a prosperous nation, and it's probably a good idea to take a close look at our prayers now and then. Ask yourself: *Do I pray more about myself than I do about others? How much time do I spend focusing on God, praising and thanking God?* God does not want you to hesitate to pray about your needs, but remember to balance your prayers with expressions of praise, thanksgiving, and love. More than anything else, this will grow your relationship with God.

QUESTION #10: Why does God let so many bad things happen?

This is a very difficult question. Even the very smartest people have not been able to answer it completely. A simple answer is that we are not meant to live here on this planet forever. We are created to live in eternity with God, where there is no sadness. This gives us something to hope for—something we can look forward to. But that doesn't make all the pain go away when bad things happen. So what can you do when bad things happen? First, you can ask God to comfort you—to help you not to feel so sad—and God promises to do it. Talk to God about how you are feeling and what you need, and God will answer your prayers. You also can ask others for help. This question is a puzzle none of us will solve before we get to heaven. Until then, we must trust God and believe that God is good and that God loves us. We know these things are true because the Bible tells us so, and because we see God's love in Jesus.

More for older children: Great thinkers through the ages have not been able to solve the dilemma presented by this question: *If God truly loves us, why does God allow there to be so much misery and pain on this earth?* Though we will never fully answer this question this side of heaven, what we can know with certainty is that God is always good. We know this because the Bible reveals God's character, showing us that God is loving, kind, caring, merciful, forgiving, compassionate, and so much more. In difficult times, turn to the Bible and study the character and the ways of God. Though you will not always understand why things happen, you will find comfort and reassurance in knowing that your God is a loving God who promises to work all things for your good.

As adult leaders in the church and in our own homes, we should hope and pray that the children in our lives will continue to ask questions about prayer for the rest of their lives. If they do, they will experience a wonderfully deep and lasting bond with God; and they will become more caring, serving, and loving persons. Many of the questions they will continue to ask do not have final or ultimate answers. That's apparently how God intends it to be. Our role is to encourage them to have a wonderful spiritual journey and to never, ever stop asking questions. Our questions are a precious gift to us from God.

II.

MAKING PRAYER CENTRAL IN WORSHIP

Weekly worship services are one of the most visible doors of entry for visitors into the life of the congregation. Whenever we gather for worship—in whatever style or setting—worship is also one of the best opportunities for guidance and teaching about a life of prayer.

As you consider the elements, flow, and tone of your own worship services in this section, you and your team will:

- Look more closely at the varied roles that prayer holds in your worship service now.
- Consider how your congregation participates in prayer as a church community and how what you pray for together as a congregation begins to define your identity.
- Learn about the importance of a variety of prayer styles to reach young and old, contemplative and active, new and seasoned worshippers.
- Identify the ways and places prayer is taught or modeled well in your worship service.
- Imagine how newcomers experience and participate in your service and look for ways to welcome and guide them.
- Make a thorough and deep exploration of the ways your worship experience helps people encounter God.

Articles:

MODELING PRAYER ON WORSHIP'S MAIN STAGE

Pamela Hawkins

Pamela Hawkins *is the editor of* Weavings, *a quarterly journal that promotes a pattern of faithful living through prayer, community, and engagement. Pam is also an ordained United Methodist pastor. In this article, she explores the role of prayer in worship and the importance of welcoming the newcomer into prayer. Through our worship experiences we are caring for the prayer life of God's people.*

Whenever God's people gather for worship, we form one of the best and most reliable opportunities to be guided in and taught about a life of prayer. We are often reminded during worship workshops that our greatest reach to the most people is through our worship life. When worship space opens, it opens to life-long members and first-time visitors; to seekers, believers, and doubters; to curious children, self-conscious parents, and discerning youth; to people who show up out of habit and others who show up in great need. But as we enter, we enter into space and time ripe for prayer. It is a space and time that every congregation, can prepare and shape for prayerful worship experiences through which all may grow in our life and depth of prayer.

Worship can serve as the "main stage" for the gathered community to experience, rehearse, and learn to pray. Through silence, words, music, images, fragrance, movement, imagination, use of light and darkness, leaders help inspire, encourage, and form the prayer lives of God's people. But before we get carried away with layers of worship planning and stage-setting, it is important to first reflect on why God's people come to worship in the first place. What are we looking for? What draws us into worship? By reflecting on these questions, we will better be able to articulate and develop our understanding of the role of prayer within the context of our worship life. Without doing so, we risk leading others through the motion of prayer with no direction.

I believe that people come to worship seeking an encounter with God. There are other reasons that people show up—expectation, coercion, curiosity, friendship. But even these are, in some way, connected with someone's search for a deeper experience of and relationship with the One whom we gather to worship.

Prayer as the language of the community is like our original tongue. Just as children . . . develop their own unique ways of expressing themselves, so our individual prayer life develops by the care of the praying community.

— Henri Nouwen

We are entrusted with both the responsibility and privilege of assisting God's people in encountering the Holy in ways that represent what we believe to be true about God made known to us in Jesus Christ. When we choose to come to a service of worship, we make a choice, in the words of the great Quaker spiritual leader Douglas Steere, to "participate, to bring our praise and honor and thanks . . . and lay them at God's feet" as part of the "humbling, enlarging, encompassing fellowship" known as the church.[22] God also desires for us to share our laments and confessions and longings when we worship. Therefore, every element of worship preparation, planning, and leadership, has the capacity to influence and help us

- **Worship is the main stage for experiencing, learning, and rehearsing prayer.**
- **Prayer is the language of worship.**
- **Language is learned through guidance and repetition.**
- **All the elements of our worship are "prayer."**
- **We are responsible for inviting, teaching, and leading the participants in prayer.**

conceive of, experience, and grow in relationship with God, whether we come in shame or joy, doubt or belief, wounded or whole.

Prayer in worship is simply one element, one practical way, one spiritual discipline that can foster and deepen this divine-human relationship; but alongside other spiritual disciplines that we embed in services of worship, prayer plays a unique and particularly significant role. Prayer is the language of worship—whatever our style, order, or tradition—it is "God-talk" and it "is of the utmost importance, because it slants and shapes our conceptions of God from early childhood."[23]

Prayer is language, whether spoken, written, embodied, sung, or rendered through image. It is, in the words of Henri Nouwen, "the language of the Christian community."[24] Still, for all the ways in which prayer language is woven through or punctuates our worship life, it will be helpful to our effectiveness as spiritual leaders and guides if we stop to remind each other that prayer is language, and that language, even our "first language," must be learned. It is the rare student who can learn a new language without steady example, clear teaching, regular practice, and frequent encouragement. We would not expect our congregation to suddenly be able to worship in French without instruction and practice. Yet, as congregational leaders, we often expect everyone in our worship service to either be fluent in, or at least "quick-studies" of, our patterns of prayer.

Two Praying Communities

I recall two worship experiences from my own past that each deeply influenced my life and leadership of prayer. The first took place during my high school years when I began to seek worship experiences that better expressed my growing sense of God's mystery than did the worship style of my home church. I visited several different congregations and worship traditions with friends.

Finally, I found a congregation whose worship seemed embroidered with God's mystery, especially through its prayers that seemed a foreign, but beautiful language to me. For several weeks I showed up, trying my best to join in their way of prayer. But after awhile, without any guidance or instruction offered from within the congregation, no matter how much I tried to learn and practice on my own, I lost confidence in my ability to learn the prayers with which I had fallen in love. No one else sitting near me Sunday after Sunday seemed to be at a loss, so I determined that prayer was probably not really the language of my life and I stopped attending that congregation, or any congregation for a few years after that.

It will be helpful to our effectiveness as spiritual leaders and guides if we stop to remind each other that prayer is language, and that language, even our "first language," must be learned.

The second experience came much later in life during my first retreat at a nearby Benedictine monastery. I arrived at the guest house just in time to unpack my car and barely get to the abbey in time to join the community for evening prayer. From the moment I stepped into the beautiful, but unfamiliar worship space, I began to feel anxious that I would not "pray" correctly or know what was expected of me by the community of monks, priests, and more experienced visitors. As eagerly as I had anticipated worshipping with the monks, a sense of panic rose in my throat and I recall planning my escape before making a complete fool of myself. But just as quickly, I felt a gentle touch on my arm. I turned to see the welcoming smile of a monk guide who led me to a seat, sat down beside me, handed me two prayer books already marked for the evening prayers, and quietly walked me through a well-worn, dog-eared order of worship that he left in my care before going to greet another uncertain visitor. To this day, in spite of the long drive to the monastery, I continue to worship and pray with this community whenever I am able.

Both congregations were praying congregations. Both had particular words, movements, patterns, and traditions of prayer specific and meaningful to their worship and communal life. But the leadership of the congregation of my youth assumed that as long as prayer was carefully woven into the fabric of worship, people would, in time, find the threads of prayer and use them. In a sense, the congregation was on its own to become a praying congregation. Prayer was indirectly taught by leadership and by insiders already fluent in the community's language, but they prayed without eye or ear for those of us trying to join them.

At the monastery, leadership made no assumptions. From the moment anyone new entered the abbey for worship, there was embodied and written guidance to prayer. New pray-ers were expected, planned for, and included. Outsiders were equipped as fresh insiders from the moment we were greeted at the door with instruction and reassurance that our prayers mattered to the congregation. In one worship setting, learning to pray was treated by leadership as a *given*. In the other, being taught how to pray was offered by leadership as a *gift*. If asked whether prayer was central to worship, I imagine congregational leaders for both communities would answer yes. But only the monks fully set worship as the main stage for God's gathered people to learn and share prayer as our "first language."

How Do We Set the Stage?

If we, too, want our congregations to grow as praying congregations, we need to set the stage, annotate the scripts, and coach the leaders so that everyone who enters can fully participate in our life of prayer. Greeters at the door, familiar with the worship details, could be certain that visitors, families with small children, or persons with hearing or mobility concerns are made aware of parts of the liturgy for which they might desire assistance. Worship leaders could review every prayer of the planned liturgy, from font size to phrase breaks to timing, with an eye and heart for the stranger or new reader. It might also be eye-opening for worship planners to look at our worship from the perspective of someone new to the faith, someone who does not know any prayers by heart, does not know the books of the Bible, does not know how to enter silence, does not know whether she is welcome at the Lord's Table. All of these elements of our worship life are, in fact, ways in which we pray together. Do we not want everyone who longs to encounter God with us to have their voice and life included with our prayers?

Where better can we teach one another the ways and words of prayer than when we gather in community, side by side, all ages and life circumstances, to worship the One in whose name we pray?

Lord, Teach Us to Pray

When Jesus' disciples, still wet behind the ears, wanted to learn to pray, he took nothing for granted in his instruction (Luke 11:1-15). He wanted them to become a praying community, a praying congregation. He knew that prayer would hold them together, especially when it seemed they were falling apart. He was not vague or patronizing or impatient. He did not leave them to figure prayer out for themselves, but instead, taught them to figure prayer into their life together. He did not assume anything, but taught them everything needed to become people of prayer.

Is this not what we desire as well? Where better can we teach one another the ways and words of prayer than when we gather in community, side by side, all ages and life circumstances, to worship the One in whose name we pray? Henri Nouwen writes, "Prayer as the language of the community is like our original tongue. Just as children . . . develop their own unique ways of expressing themselves, so our individual prayer life develops by the care of the praying community."[25] May we, through our worship, attend to and care for the prayer life of the people of God.

Ideas to Consider

- If worship is the main stage for teaching prayer, what are you presenting on stage?
- How do your opening moments set the tone of worship each week?
- Can you name three ways that the practice of prayer is taught in your weekly worship services to newcomers?
- Invite a friend from another congregation, perhaps a different denomination, to visit your service. Is your visitor able to fully participate and follow the order of service? Where are the obstacles or surprises?
- How are children prepared to enter worship with confidence? Do you offer a preparation class, a take-home family booklet, or even a tape or CD of prayers or creeds recited in worship?

ALL OF WORSHIP AS PRAYER

K. C. Ptomey

K. C. Ptomey *was the senior pastor of Westminster Presbyterian Church for over twenty years. He is now the Louis H. and Katherine S. Zbinden Professor of Pastoral Ministry and Leadership at Austin Presbyterian Theological Seminary in Austin, Texas. Here, he writes about striving to make each service an opportunity to encounter God.*

When I started my pastorate at Westminster Presbyterian Church in Nashville a number of years ago, we began planning an annual three-day staff retreat around various programmatic topics and strategic questions. It was what you might call "end-of-the-rope" planning. After a few years, we realized there was little left for us to cover, so we began to focus on our own faith formation as leaders. We did spiritual personality assessments and brought in strong resource people such as Bob Hughes, Ben Curtis, and Marjorie Thompson to lead our sessions.

One year we had Tom Ward teach us about centering prayer. Three times a day for three days, we sat in silence. We would gather in silence, read a psalm, and then sit for twenty minutes in silent prayer. We were reminded that we live in a world filled with noise and activity, and that listening in silence is a very important exercise missing from most of our lives. We discovered that when we understand prayer as listening and being open to God in silence, we begin to see prayer as an overall openness to the Spirit of God—not merely as words or requests.

During these retreats, we began to ask ourselves, "What would it mean for the life of the congregation if we included silence in worship?" This question prompted a vision for an experiment.

An Experiment: Creating Space for Silence in Worship

Following one retreat, we decided to add silence to the worship service in an unannounced way—without any explanation. We began with the aspects of the service that I, as pastor, could control. Though I couldn't easily influence the pace of those portions of the service involving music and sung responses, I was able to control the parts of the service that I led, which included the Prayer of Illumination, the reading of the Scripture, the homily, and the Prayers of the People. So I began to include an extended silence before the Prayer for Illumination, and after the homily, under the rubric: A Moment of Meditation. Also, at the beginning of the Prayers of the People, after calling the congregation to prayer, the liturgist would inject an extended period of silence. Although it was unannounced, people noticed. I began to get questions and comments. In my morning men's Bible study, I'd hear, "Hey, last Sunday I had to open my eyes to see if you'd fallen asleep up there!" Similar comments and questions let us know that our strategy was providing opportunities for teaching and communication—an open door for talking about prayer and silence and the need to build in time for listening to God in worship.

Effects of the Experiment

As we continued observing the extended silences in worship, we began to hear more conversations within the congregation that provided opportunities to engage in dialogue about prayer and silence. We acknowledged that God knows our needs before we ask, and that prayer is primarily about listening and being open to God. In the midst of these discussions, difficult questions about prayer began to surface, questions such as "What about unanswered prayer?"; "How does prayer affect healing?"; and "Why am I not getting the answers I am requesting?" As we attempted to probe the depths of these questions together, we affirmed that although there is great mystery surrounding them all, each question leads back to the understanding that prayer is more about listening for what God is trying to say than it is about getting what we want.

The apostle Paul speaks of praying without ceasing. This is no answer to the perplexing unanswered questions about prayer that trouble us all: "Why are some of my prayers not answered? Why does God never speak to me directly? What's the point of prayer anyway?" Our Lord himself was a person of prayer who admonished his followers to pray and taught us how to do so—all of which suggests that prayer is an essential of the spiritual life, an indispensable element in our relationship with God even as our troubling, unanswered questions remain. These ruminations led our staff and many of our parishioners to conclude that more important than intellectualizing about prayer may be adopting a discipline of silence: prayer as listening to God rather than speaking to God.

Next Steps Toward More Silence and "Space" for Listening in Worship

In light of the positive outcomes of the extended silences experiment, we began an effort to interpret all of worship as a time of listening to and being open to God. We reexamined the Prayers of the People, our intercessory prayer time that follows the homily. In earlier years, our service, like many Protestant services, included a "pastoral prayer." This was essentially an opportunity for the pastor to rehash the sermon message using great eloquence—to verbally "dust the stars." Typically this prayer included thanksgiving, praise, confession, intercession, and supplication. When our denominational prayer book was revised in the early 1990's, the Pastoral Prayer took on a new shape and name: the

Prayers of the People became a prayer of intercession and supplication. Because the Service of the Lord's Day includes prayers of adoration, confession, and thanksgiving, the Prayers of the People could be focused purely on intercession. A byproduct was the elimination of redundancy in the service.

Early in my tenure as pastor, the Worship Committee in recognition of the fact that "liturgy" means, literally, "the work of the people," decided to invite laity in the church to participate in writing the Sunday services. We wanted worship to truly become "the work of the people." But because some people are more facile with words and more poetic than others, we recognized the need to choose carefully those who would be writing liturgy. So, we worked to have a teacher or attorney or others with expertise in the spoken and written word to work on each liturgy team. The teams wrote the prayers and responses of the Sunday services, or they accessed the rich liturgical resources of our heritage. Typically members of the liturgy teams did not also serve as liturgists. The clergy and some carefully chosen lay persons with gifts for public speaking actually led worship.

As we talked with the first lay liturgy team, we came up with some basic ideas:

- The liturgy can have more space and silence and less verbiage.
- Our goal is more listening and less talking.
- Some of the best prayers are already written; we can draw on the great writers across time.

Rather than the liturgy being eloquent, we wanted it to express more authentic communication with God. The goal was to be open to God's voice. We instructed the lay leaders to model through these corporate prayers that prayer is not about having all the right words. This offered worshippers great freedom and relief. It communicated that prayer is not demonstrating verbal skill but coming into the Holy Presence (Isaiah 6).

Extending Silence Into Other Parts of the Service

What had begun as a simple experiment had now blossomed into a full-flown effort to revise the pace of the service, allowing more silence and space for listening to God. Working with the choir on the timing of the service was a natural partnership. Music leaders and musicians understand the effectiveness of pauses or rests, varying dynamics, and pace. Now they had a new opportunity for leading in worship—an opportunity to create more space for listening. Others, such as lay readers, had to train themselves in slowing the pace. Observing extended silences and allowing more space throughout the service for reflection has not become easy for most worshippers. This is dramatic evidence that in our culture, spiritual discipline does not come easily or naturally to most.

There are signs of encouragement. People sometimes complain that the time for silent confession following the Prayer of Confession and preceding the sung response is too short. Depending upon who is involved in leading the service on a given Sunday, I instruct the leaders either to actually time the silences or simply look to one of the pastors for the nod of the head indicating when to move on to the next reading.

The Ultimate Goal: Encountering God

In the time our congregation utilized lay liturgy teams, over 150 people of our 700 worshippers served on a writing team. This created a better-informed and educated congregation. More people in worship have an appreciation of the order of service and the subtleties of the liturgical experience; and more people have begun to embrace the concept that all of worship is prayer—a time for listening and being open to God.

As we grew into these changes, we wondered how our service format would appeal to visitors and new members. We had made, as a congregation, a clear decision to do traditional worship. We included global music from Taizé to African styles and had variety in the service, but we did not include contemporary elements in worship such as "praise" bands or projection on screens of the words of hymns or the liturgy. We found that our growing edge continued to be young families—people in their 30s and 40s often with young children. In membership classes, we heard again and again this message: "We feel the need for roots for ourselves and our children." We also heard that the liturgy made sense and, most significantly, that these new worshippers came away feeling they had experienced an encounter with God.

Prayer loops of peaceful images and Scripture verses viewed on a projection screen invite worshippers to ease into a time of meditation and personal communion with God.

On the DVD-Rom, you'll find some prayer loops that you can use in your congregation.

Encountering God is the ultimate goal of worship and prayer alike. Our desire is not only to make prayer central in worship; it also is to communicate that all of worship is prayer, because prayer is simply being in communion with God. As we embrace this understanding of prayer and worship, all of life becomes prayer. When we pray and worship, the important question is not, "Did I feel good?" or "Did I enjoy it?" but, "Did I have an encounter with God?"

Ideas to Consider

6 Keys to Making All of Worship Prayer
1. Understand the worship experience as an encounter with God.
2. Pay attention to both language and silence.
3. Remember that silence is as important as words and music.
4. Create space in worship for listening and being open to God.
5. Involve lay people in worship leadership.
6. Make it your goal to be constantly shaped in the direction of a praying people.

AN INVITATION TO COMMUNE WITH GOD

K. C. Ptomey

Our congregation observed Holy Communion at the beginning of every quarter as well as on the first Sunday of every new church season and Easter Sunday. The prayers spoken during this service were a major part of coming to the Communion table. Prayer is being in communion with God.

As we began to increase the frequency of our Communion celebrations, one of the church elders said to me, "Pastor, since we started having Communion so often, every time I sit down at a table, I think about it." Indeed, every table is a communion table and an invitation to commune with God.

THE PRIVILEGE OF CORPORATE PRAYER

Kim Thomas

Kim Thomas, *with her husband, Jim, pastors The Village Chapel in Nashville, Tennessee. She is also a painter and a published author. In this article, Kim describes the challenge of making corporate prayer meaningful in worship and small groups, all in a congregation experiencing many new forms of worship and ministry.*

The discipline of inner stillness is difficult to cultivate in a crowd. Corporate prayer brings with it several challenges, but the need for silence, one's inward places being stilled enough to transverse the ground before the feet of heaven, is a uniquely ambitious necessity. To simultaneously still hundreds of people, with needs and restless longings, to be quiet together for one unified purpose . . . well, that is the privilege and challenge of corporate prayer in our Sunday services.

The ragged collection of image bearers park in the lots and streets nearby our 100-year-old adopted convent. This charming remnant of the nuns of St. Bernard school has become the perfect environment for our blooming congregation. Our church phrase has been "The Village Chapel: New forms for ancient truths." What better kind of building to house such a community of faith than an ancient religious institution repurposed for new things?

We believe that prayer is an essential element of engaging with God, both on an individual and corporate level. So in our quest for new forms for ancient truths, we tried to creatively offer opportunities to encourage corporate prayer. We had the requisite forty or fifty candles, and a printed page of directed topics for prayer, and we encouraged people to take turns covering the topics. I hosted women's nights, where we prayed for each person to our left, silent or out loud, squeezing their hand signifying "Amen," and the prayer passed to the next woman. After the tragic 2004 tsunami, we huddled together with prayers for the needs of the children left orphaned. We lit candles and spoke sentence prayers together on a Thursday night one spring; the next quarter we prayed our confessions, symbolically placing our sin at the cross by hanging individual chains on a rebar cross suspended in the middle of the room;

As we stumbled in our good intentions, simplicity was to be our best tool.

the next time we wrote private needs on papers, then passed a tall silver compote around the room and each took a folded paper and prayed for what was written on it.

And each time, the crowd was smaller than the time before.

79

Our attempts at incorporating prayer into the life of The Village Chapel were not instant fits. As we stumbled in our good intentions, simplicity was to be our best tool. Our group took to having coffee during the service, following worship leaders who remained seated and inconspicuous, and placing their tithes and offerings in a bucket near the door rather than in passed plates. If they could adapt and respond to these new forms, perhaps new forms for our prayer life were simply too many new forms. So, we resorted to an "old school" approach for our prayer ministry: We began a prayer chain.

I must say that I believe that was where the heart first beat in our church's prayer experience. Many years before, there were telephone prayer chains, the new form we did choose to use was email. (Read more about The Village Chapel's prayer request system on page 130.)

I believe that part of what has worked for our group is that we have some ... order to the experience, but we pray as if we are just one or two. One of us speaks for all of us, but all of us unite our hearts and attention to the needs of those among us.

Sacred emails, blessed stories of thanksgiving, of aches and sufferings, collections of the broken and the lost, the willing and the interceded for, the known and the unknown, have been at the foundation of building our corporate prayer experience at The Village Chapel. And as is the case for many things done by the quiet urging of the Spirit, somewhere along the way, we began to pray the weekly prayer lists in our Sunday services too. We didn't assemble a team to research the best way to incorporate prayer in the services, we didn't install a kneeling rail, make pillows, light candles, or play the sound track from "Chant" behind the prayers—we simply and faithfully began to pray for the needs in an unhurried and caring way.

I believe that part of what has worked for our group is that we have some organization and order to the experience, but we pray as if we are just one or two. One of us speaks for all of us, but all of us unite our hearts and attention to the needs of those among us. When I am leading, I almost forget that there are hundreds in the room with me, once my eyes are closed or are on the list of concerns sitting on the little music stand that serves as our podium.

I usually begin my prayer with a personal prayer, for something to set my heart in line with where it should be. Like: "Disturb me, God, from my lethargic and numb state of weekly wear, and restore a heart of care and tenderness that I might know you again." Or I might note the weekly weather, and how God used all of His supplies in providing thunderstorms, lightening, rain, and yet blue skies, and cool breezes, and fresh earth responded in blooms and sprouts. I thank God that in the ocean of people, He still knows me as one drop among the deep, by name. I confess that the self-hyphenated sins of self-sufficiency, self-absorption, self-destruction, and self-focus have interrupted my progress at trust, faith, and surrender. I ask God to slow my breathing and anxious thoughts, that my connection to God would be unhurried and unfrazzled. I thank God that He is the author of all goodness, and all that is beautiful, and that He offers us the privilege of knowing Him, and I celebrate that greatest joy of joys: that God would be KNOWN! I beg God to again seize us with His great affection, and then thank Him that He allows His throne room to also be an emergency room, and I begin to bring the wounded before God in short but specific detailed fashion.

Some weeks, I instruct the congregation to get comfortable, to take a deep breath, to prepare for a season of focused prayer—in other words, *this may take a while*. So far, they have not been restless or anxious, and the time is sacredly still, somehow, divinely orchestrated, and our hearts synchronize. Like a smooth ballet of ebb and flow, the words of my mouth and the meditations of their hearts find their way as incense to the throne room, and our heavenly Father receives each request with the loving and able arms of the Author of All. I so often feel the weight of the broken *shalom*, the heaviness of the need, and like Flannery O'Connor's Mrs. Greenleaf, my heart rocks back and forth over the needs as I symbolically kneel in submission, leaving the written, spoken, and unspoken requests before God. And by the time my lips find "Amen," and we have surrendered to "Thy will be done," my heart is strangely warmed, uplifted, and ready to sing in worship again.

This is the story of prayer at The Village Chapel, three services on Sunday, and throughout the week. I believe that when the requests are prayed over, if you find yourself not simply the message carrier, but instead the Lord allows you to *be* the one with the mother in the hospital, or with the child who is prodigal, or with the friend in need of work, or the husband who has lost his way, if you can find your way to being IN their needs, your prayer becomes less strained and the words come faster than you can speak them.

What a privilege to lead, be led, and participate in corporate prayer each Sunday with those who gather in our repurposed chapel. To partner with and be the voice of the voiceless, or the tired and weary, is an honor beyond measure, *soli deo gloria*.

Ideas to Consider

- How do you invite the congregation into a time of prayer within the service?
- At The Village Chapel, email is used to bring the real prayers of the people into the community prayer. How do prayer requests reach the worship service for you?

- Kim describes leading prayer in worship as "one speaking for all, uniting all hearts."
- What ways can the prayer requests be woven into meaningful corporate prayer?
- Where could you simplify? Do you have changes in style, timing, or technology that cause your team, like The Village Chapel leaders, to look for simplicity or known traditions in leading prayer?

THREE PRAYERS

Kim Thomas

Our Father.
There is one who knows my name.
But knows me more by the whispers of my soul. In my scattered silence, He fills up the quiet with stirrings that have no words. He sees my blemishes and acknowledges them, but encourages my intention beyond my ability. When there is a coming among, I am even more sure of His firm hold on me. I open my mouth and before the word is formed on my lips another says "Father" and the elements of life and heaven are corporately called into the moment, enjoining us in the commonality of the divine. No longer merely a consumer of God, I am now a communer with God. And I am persuaded.

Who art in heaven.
No steaming engine or flight by wing can travel to this place. There is no transport by turning wheels or simplicity of will. It is for now a transport of spirit for we still are tethered by flesh and blood. In an ever-forward, ever-upward direction we are drawn. To dismiss heaven as simply a lovely thought would only expose our impatience with what we don't know. For now it is enough to know that heaven is where the Father-of-all dwells, with every remembrance and every perhaps.

Hallowed be thy name.
Exploding from heaven in the form of providential visitations is the Acknowledged One. Ever watching, ever making, ever shaping. Transcendent, recognized, yet skinless. Limitless, beautiful, but beyond comprehension. My brain swirls as holiness fizzes up through port. The earth's relentless turning is a flimsy attempt at time passing in comparison with the steady fire that burns in perpetual foreverness. Carry the weary to the gate. Lean one finger towards His exquisite honor, pull away, and find yourself upside down in awkward awe.

"Give Us This Day Our Daily Bread"

Becca Stevens

The Rev. Becca Stevens *is an Episcopal priest at St. Augustine's Chapel on the Vanderbilt University campus. She is the founder of Magdalene, a residential community for women with a criminal history of prostitution and drug abuse. In his article, Becca describes how both praying with a community can support and sustain us through seasons when we cannot pray for ourselves. She also looks at the role traditional and repetitive prayers can play, helping us when finding new words is a struggle.*

There was a couple who came to the church I pastored for years. They were faithful members and everyone loved them. After she died, while he kept attending church, the way he worshipped changed. He would come in a few minutes after the service started then sit in the back and leave after he had taken Communion. No one questioned him, just gave him the time and space he needed to mourn his beloved. A long time afterwards, he told me that for months after her death he just couldn't pray. He didn't feel exactly anger at God, he knew that death was part of the gift of life, he just didn't feel anything. He didn't have a lot of faith and didn't have enough energy to fake the words in prayers that he didn't feel.

His confession about his lack of faith was very tender and loving. Then he explained that what he had felt good about was coming to the chapel and sitting with the people who knew her and letting them pray for him. It was comforting to him during his grief that he didn't have to pray, but that because of the structure of the liturgy other people could literally pray for him. He could sit in the pew and let their prayers wash over him and as their familiar words were offered up, it connected him to a faith he had known.

Many of the prayers we offer in our congregations are for the sake of the whole community. We pray for those who cannot pray for themselves; we pray for those who are suffering; for those who feel alone; for those oppressed in mind, body, and spirit; and we pray that all of our faiths will increase through these common prayers.

Finally the man told me that the previous Sunday had been the first time since her death that he actually prayed the common prayers printed in the bulletin. He had felt the strength coming back in his breath, and that it was now his turn to pick up the communal prayer and pray for others who were grieving or just too worn down to feel a genuine prayer. Now that he was feeling connected, those same prayers that comforted him and fed him, he was offering for love of others in the community.

His beautiful parable sums up pretty well why we need communal prayers that we offer up as congregations. We as individuals are not always inspired or capable; we don't always believe what it is we know we are supposed to pray. The communal liturgies that hold old sacred prayers offer us a structure, a history, and a way of holding each other together through joyous times and heartbreaks. The prayers that we know in our hearts are the prayers that can carry us through our lives, and they are also the prayers that we can offer to carry others through.

> **Christ's Spirit is praying within us even when we lack both the wisdom and the words for prayer. Although we may not know God's will on a given issue, the Spirit within us surely does. In other words, our most immature prayers have an inbuilt self-corrective. Though we feel ignorant in our prayers, the Spirit does not. Though we feel exhausted and confused, the Spirit does not. Though we feel lacking in faith, the Spirit does not. God is not so far off that we need to raise our voices to be heard. We need only groan.**[26]
> *— Philip Yancey*

Jesus himself offered us a common prayer to be used when we gather. I have recited that prayer for as long as I can remember. "Our father, who art in heaven," we still say weekly before we take the consecrated bread. Sometimes I say that prayer and drift off in my mind, thinking about something else all together. It is a blessing to me sometimes that much of what I say weekly is repetition that can bore me and free my mind to travel and resolve things that are stirring my heart. Sometimes I say that prayer and think about the act of praying and what it means to be faithful. I think about how my mom and dad said the same prayer and how I said the prayer recently to a friend who was passing. I think about how some say *debt* and some say *trespass* and wonder how and when it changed. And then, every so often, I say that prayer that I have recited a hundred thousand times and something new speaks to me. A phrase like "give us this day our daily bread" catches me and sinks to a new, deep place in me and reforms me. All of the sudden I am filled again with new gratitude for this prayer that held words that were not dressed up for others, but instead were words that stripped me down to my core and allowed me to grow in my faith. I remember that I have not been faithful and have been needing years of bread stored to feel safe. I remember that I can give so much more away, that I have my daily bread already.

We do not pray the prayers we believe; we pray what we hope to someday believe. That is the nature of prayer, that it will form and shape our journey, so it makes sense that the words can't all come from us, and that we would offer them as a community of faith, making the journey together, just like the disciples.

Years ago I founded a program called Magdalene that serves women coming off the streets with criminal histories of violence, addiction, and prostitution. We wanted to offer sanctuary and be a testimony to the truth that in the end love and grace are the most powerful forces for change in the world. Every Monday, Wednesday, and Friday for the past twelve years we have gathered in a circle to pray and reflect.

We do not pray the prayers we believe; we pray what we hope to someday believe. That is the nature of prayer, that it will form and shape our journey.

There were probably about eight of us in the circle when we began in 1997. There was never a worship leader in the circle, and we didn't have a common prayer book. What has been fascinating to me is how naturally, slowly, and surely a liturgy has developed and become the safe place for a larger and larger group of women and people in the community. There are usually close to fifty people a week gracing the circle at present. The ritual has become that someone reads a meditation from the twelve step tradition, then we go around the circle and people can take a minute to offer a prayer, give thanks, or tell a story. Finally, one person in the circle closes with the Lord's Prayer. It is one of the sweetest circles to sit in. You will see women who graduated years ago come back and weep when the circle gets to them. You will hear women volunteers talk about the gift of the circle and what it means to believe they can heal. You will feel the force of communal prayer shifting individuals and the power of gratitude fill us all again, like it was the first time we have sat in that space.

There is renewed interest in congregations all over the country for old liturgies like *lecto divina* and the Taizé prayers. People find reassurance and depth in going back and letting old ideas fill them, instead of

We don't have to wow each other with our deep thoughts or new insights; we just pray over and over the words given to us, and let them wash over us and form us.

filling themselves with new ideas. Congregations are discovering that being bound by old liturgies and common prayers actually frees them to experience new ideas and new depths of faith. It is like being well-grounded enables us to move more freely in our faith. It is our history, and it gives us a path we can walk on and deviate from. It is our common faith, and it gives us a place to push up against and a structure to build upon. Being a part of a community that recites creed and says the Lord's Prayer doesn't mean that everyone in the congregation is able to recite it all without doubts, it means that together we know where we come from and that these prayers can hold us in a common bond as a community of faith.

Common prayers recited together are essential to our lives of faith and ensure that communal worship doesn't center on a pastor's ability to create worship. Sometimes I feel like a congregation is waiting to be entertained or at least to be moved by my sermon. As soon as the sermon is over and we begin the prayers of the people, you can feel a shift in the worship. We become a congregation, not an entertainer and audience, and we are bound together in worship. It may feel less dramatic because it is scripted, but it is what is life-giving and bonding in the service. The prayers are owned by all of us. We don't individually have to wow each other with our deep thoughts or new insights; we just pray over and over the words given to us, and let them wash over us and form us.

Ideas to Consider

- How do you use traditional common prayers in your service now? What benefits do you currently see in reciting familiar prayers in worship? Are there other opportunities these could bring you?
- How does this role of the well-known prayer mirror the value of silence mentioned in the article "All of Worship as Prayer" by K. C. Ptomey (see page 74)?

EXPERIENTIAL PRAYER IN WORSHIP

Stacy Hood

Stacy Hood *is Director of Worship Ministries for Grace Community United Methodist Church in Shreveport, Louisiana. She works with the creative ministry team and over 300 volunteers in music, sound, multimedia, drama, altar ministry, dance, and youth worship-related ministries In this article, Stacy offers three tangible ways congregations can respond through prayer to local and global events.*

At age two, she takes her cue: "Mary Clare, let's pray." With hands clasped tightly, eyes closed, and face scrunched, she bows her head. A closer look as she prays reveals beautiful blue eyes peeking out from behind her eyelids to make sure everyone else is still participating in the ritual. From Hollywood movie sets to dinner tables set in suburbia USA, "Every head bowed and every eye closed" is the common visual image American culture generally associates with the act of prayer. While a reflective and silent form of prayer is richly valued, worship offers the opportunity to model multiple expressions of meaningful prayer experiences.

Many people are kinesthetic learners; movement enhances the learning process. In the same way, some people are kinesthetic prayers; movement enhances the prayer experience. Lighting candles, touching water to remember one's baptism, writing a prayer to place on the altar, or praying while viewing a series of images on a screen are all active expressions of prayer that can serve as meaningful experiences in worship.

A form of prayer found to be particularly meaningful at Grace Community United Methodist Church in Shreveport, Louisiana, is an active prayer that has a tangible component for those *in* worship and those *outside* the walls of the church who are the objects of that prayer. Providing a tangible prayer experience allows people to connect at the point of touch; working together toward a common goal to create something lasting.

Prayer in Response to Events

In the aftermath of terror strikes and hurricanes and other natural disasters, people often feel there is nothing that can be done to help in such a situation. Images of devastation are replayed on the television screen while many people watch and pray, "Lord, please help those people through this horrible situation." While the prayers are sincere, many hearts are left with a desire to make a tangible difference in the lives of those in critical need. Others struggle to process how prayer makes a difference in the lives of those for whom they pray. "How do I know my prayer for a starving child in another country or in my own neighborhood makes a difference?"

The following three examples will demonstrate acts of prayer in worship that reach beyond the walls of the church in a tangible way. Allowing a congregation to participate in tangible forms of prayer offers an experience of prayer that will continue long after that sweet hour of worship has passed.

A Health Kit Prayer

The United Methodist Committee on Relief (UMCOR) is one of the most organized and effective agencies touching lives globally. The tools provided by UMCOR allow individuals and local churches to participate in God's unfolding work throughout the world. The health kit opportunity provided on UMCOR's website (www.umcor.org) can become an active prayer experience in worship that has a tangible component that allows for the congregation to work together toward a common goal to create something lasting.

How Do We Do It?

UMCOR clearly defines the items needed and the way in which a health kit—a plastic bag containing basic items such as a washcloth and a toothbrush—is to be assembled (http://new.gbgm-umc.org/umcor/getconnected/supplies/health-kit/). The cost of the items for the health kit is dependent upon the preparation time your team is willing to contribute. Searching for discounted items can reduce the cost of this project. Well-known chain stores are often willing to reduce their price or donate items if asked in advance. This can be a pricey project if someone makes a run to the local drug store the day before worship. Advanced planning accompanied by a bargain hunter will make this a financially affordable prayer experience.

Preparing the worship area for this project will vary with each congregation. Consider, however, the flow your congregation uses for Communion. People often come forward row by row to receive Communion. By placing the items down either side of the Communion rails, people may walk forward, pick up each item needed, and return to their seats to assemble the kit. For those unable to come forward, ushers can gather and deliver the items. With a clear explanation and demonstration of how the congregation will move together to make this project happen, this prayerful project is smoothly executed.

People need to have a clear understanding of how these kits will be used. Whether assembled during a time when a natural disaster has just occurred or in preparation for future emergencies, it is important for people to understand that what they are prayerfully doing will make a substantial difference in the life of another human being or community. The pastor or other leader responsible for framing this prayer project must cast a vision for the difference the seemingly small act will make in the lives of hundreds of people. Mentally walking people through what it would be like to lose a home, an entire city, or to be relocated miles from home with nothing but the clothes one is wearing can help people imagine a situation where the health kits might be used. Ask the congregation to imagine enduring three or four days with no toothbrush or washcloth. Then ask the congregation to imagine being handed a health kit— a kit that will provide a sense of comfort in a devastating situation. Ask them to imagine God's love surrounding the person who receives a health kit. Framing the way in which the health kit will meet the needs of people in difficult situations will allow this prayerful activity to strengthen the congregation's ability to see with "other-centered" eyes.

As the kits are assembled, it may be helpful to provide a guide for individual prayer. You may wish to have someone verbally guide the assembly time. You might use instrumental music encouraging people to pray silently. A simple statement might be projected which states: "Lord, though we do not know the destination of this kit or the person who will be touched by this kit, we pray that the recipient will feel a touch of Your love and grace. We pray that the hope we find in You, O God, might be felt by the ones who will receive these health kits." It is important to assume that not all persons are aware of how to pray "actively."

Once the kits have been assembled, have the congregation stand, holding the health kits, and have someone pray over the health kits. Have the congregation follow the same path for coming forward and place the health kits on or near the altar. It is effective to have a familiar hymn for corporate singing as people physically bring forward the prayer-filled gift that has been prepared. Including personal notes in the health kits is prohibited, but there is no limit to the amount of prayer that can be directed toward those who will be receiving the kits in a time of brokenness and need.

Regardless of the size of a congregation, it will always be easier to get a smaller group of people to assemble the health kits. In fact, someone will probably question why this activity cannot be taken care of quickly and efficiently outside of worship! Use this type of response to help shape church leadership's understanding of how important it is for the entire congregation to engage in God's unfolding work in the world. This one act of prayer and outreach might encourage someone to take a deeper step into other prayer or mission moments in the future. Allowing people to actively engage in prayerful work might help to change the way in which an individual approaches life's daily tasks. The completion of the health kits is a tool for spiritual growth for the congregation as much as it is an offering of hope for those in need.

Reflecting upon the incorporation of this activity into worship at Grace Community, I am reminded of the way in which the oldest of hands and the youngest of hands worshipfully worked and prayed together. Planning worship that provides "handles" for the 7-year-old and the 70-year-old can be difficult. Maybe it is in the act of corporate prayer, in the art of hands-on mission, and through the sensitivity to the needs of society both locally and globally, that worship can be transformative across generational lines.

A Handwritten Prayer

This same sense of multigenerational cohesiveness could be felt at Grace Community the weekend after planes flew into the Twin Towers and the Pentagon, forever changing history. As worship services filled with people in shock and disbelief, searching for hope in a time of fear and grief, an opportunity to engage in active and tangible prayer was offered to all those who gathered. This was a situation where replayed images via news media left people asking the question, "Lord, please help us through this situation; what can we do to reach out to those struggling at Ground Zero?" Though it has been several years since 9/11, the particular form of prayer used in the aftermath of this historic event might be meaningful in a variety of future situations affecting congregations at the local, state, national, or global level.

How Did We Do It?

As children came forward for Children's Time, they were allowed time to process the events of the past few days; to retell the story from their own perspective and ask questions. This time with the children turned into a reflection upon those killed and injured in New York City and elsewhere, and on the amazing firefighters, police officers, and other people working hard to save as many people as possible. Instead of dismissing the children, Children's Time continued for the rest of the service as children were handed crayons and blank sheets of paper. Stretched out across the floor in the front of the worship area, children quietly created beautiful cards to send to those persons working long, hard hours at Ground Zero. The service continued as they prayed a prayer of thanks and hope through their crayons.

A similar process unfolded for youth and adults. The music and message allowed people to worship and experience a God of hope in fearful and uncertain times while providing a tangible means of prayer to offer God's hope to others. As part of the sermon for this service, youth and adults were handed paper and pencils to write prayers of hope and encouragement to be sent to those sitting in shelters and medical clinics in New York City. Each handwritten prayer would be rolled up and tied with yarn to a small hand-carved cross, prayerfully created by a wood carver in the congregation. The writing of the prayers, the carving of the wood, and the colorful images of children allowed the congregation to engage in tangible prayer which offered a touch of God's reconciling work in the world to people in need.

Navigating the logistics of such an activity in worship is fairly easy:

1. Blank paper and crayons are passed out to children during Children's Time.
2. Blank index cards or small sheets of paper can be inserted in bulletins for use by youth and adults while ushers distribute pencils at the appropriate time in the service.
3. A sample prayer, either projected or printed in the bulletin, provides guidance for people who have not had a previous occasion to write a prayer. Encouraging people to sign the prayers with only a first name or from "a member of YOUR CHURCH NAME" is recommended.
4. Each individual situation will guide the inclusion of something, such as the wooden crosses in this example. The particular situation and the gifts of those within your own congregation will help determine what is right for your situation.
5. Allowing people to move forward to place the prayers on or near the altar, similar to the way in which the health kits were brought forward, is meaningful for the congregation. Providing feedback to the congregation as to the way in which these prayers touched the lives of people in difficult situations (and you will receive feedback in unexpected and surprising ways) will affirm the way in which God is working in and through each member to offer hope to the world.

A Backpack Prayer

Allowing intentional prayer to surround the rhythms of our culture helps people to focus on allowing prayer to permeate the activities of daily life. One may follow the Christian Year in planning worship, but one must walk alongside the ebb and flow of the public educational calendar as well. "Back to School" for our society is approached by many with the same sense of renewal as found on New Year's Day. How is it that an active and tangible form of prayer in worship can allow children and adults to feel affirmed, cared for, and prayed for as they continue to love God and neighbor, participating in God's reconciling work in the world, as they move through the educational year?

Children and teachers alike carry backpacks or bags to school. Designate a particular worship service for children, youth, teachers, and other school personnel to bring a backpack or bag with them to worship. Encourage other members of the congregation to bring a backpack for a child in the community unable to purchase a backpack. During the designated prayer time in the service have everyone with a bag come forward to the altar area. Have a special prayer, either led by an individual(s) or by inclusion of the entire congregation, which offers words of peace, protection, safety, endurance, and joy for those who will participate in the new school year. At the conclusion of the prayer, ushers should be ready to pass out luggage tags to those standing in the front of the worship space. These tags will hang on the bags as a reminder not only of God's love and grace, but as a reminder of the love and support of the worshipping community. As people return to be seated, those who brought backpacks to be blessed for other children in the community may place them at the foot of the altar. Direct the congregation's attention to the bookmark inserted in the bulletin and ask them to use it as a reminder to pray for the children and teachers during the school year.

How Did We Do It?

At Grace Community you will find a "Blessing of the Backpacks" article online and in the bulletin at the end of July as preparations begin for this active and tangible prayer that will occur the weekend before the school year begins. Prior to this announcement, communication materials would have been in place for several weeks encouraging people to purchase backpacks for children in our neighboring community who will not have backpacks for the new school year. This is a great way to involve those without children or empty-nesters to feel included in this prayer experience. Luggage tags will be created on inexpensive paper and laminated. The tag will contain a short prayer and/or Scripture as a reminder to each student and teacher that his or her faith community is praying for them during the school year. "The people of YOUR CHURCH NAME love you and are praying for you," is a simple example. Additional luggage tags will be made available for several weeks to those children or adults who may have been out of town during the special time of prayer. These tags can be attached to the bags in a variety of ways depending on the budget for the activity. (The bargain hunter needed for the health kit activity might come in handy here also!)

This type of active and tangible prayer in worship can be an incredible community-building process for a congregation. If you find yourself reading this, thinking to yourself, "This won't work in my congregation as we don't have any children or youth," then stop and imagine what a powerful opportunity this would be if your congregation participated in this form of prayer, focusing on the part of the prayer that includes children in the community who cannot afford a backpack. Again, the blessing here would be for those in the worship service and those outside the walls of the church.

Ideas to Consider

- As a diverse people, we participate in diverse prayer experiences in worship so that all God's children might encounter God in a powerful way.
- As you reflect on these three examples of prayer experiences in worship, what other active and tangible forms of prayer might you, and those who design worship in your congregation, work together to provide in your worship services over the next year?

CHILDREN'S PRAYER IN WORSHIP

Barbara E. Davis

Barbara E. Davis, *ordained in the United Church
of Christ, is the Minister of
Christian Education at the
First Presbyterian Church in
New York City, where she has
served for eleven years. She
gives oversight to the educational programming for
children, youth, and adults,
as well as various other
pastoral responsibilities.
Here, Barbara describes her
experience with engaging
children in a time of prayer
during worship and
offers two examples of
children's prayers.*

Creating a time to pray with children in worship is a meaningful way for our younger members to fully participate in the worship life of the church. There was a time in our congregation when children did not participate in Sunday morning worship at all but went right to their Sunday morning activities. In our growing Greenwich Village congregation, with many young families, we needed a way to worship with our children in a real and significant way.

Our solution was not the more traditional "children's sermon" but a children's prayer near the beginning of the service. For twelve years now we have been having a special children's prayer time about ten minutes into the service, just after the first lesson. Our congregation worships in a beautiful, eight-hundred-seat sanctuary with a lovely elevated platform reached by spacious marble steps. Although beautiful, the area of worship can feel removed from the people. When it's time for prayer, we call the children to come to the front of the sanctuary and gather on the stairs. The pastoral staff come down and gather with the children for prayer. The prayers themselves are short—about two minutes long.

As Minister of Christian Education, I usually write the prayers and lead the children during this special time. I try to keep the prayers relevant, dealing with topics the children are thinking about such as the seasons of the year, events in the world, and their families and pets. We begin with a prayer for the world and then move on to the theme for the day. Our theme might be the liturgical season or a topic such as forgiveness or sharing. We then ask God to remember and to be with all the people who are sick or lonely. If we have church members who are ill, we include them by name in the prayer at this time. We always end this portion of our prayer by reminding one another that God isn't just with us here in church but is with us throughout the week, perhaps using a phrase such as, "Remember as you go forth from here that God is with you." Then we conclude our prayer time by praying the Lord's Prayer together.

We've seen lasting benefits from this time in our congregation. The children's prayer is simple and short, and its very format opens up prayer for the adults as well as the children. Many say it's their favorite time in the service. In other congregations where our staff members have served, "children's time" has almost always been enjoyable and positive. Adults want to see the children during this special time. But we want participants and worshippers rather than observers. So, this time of prayer has given more meaning and a sense of true worship to this time with the children.

The most difficult part of making the prayer time successful is keeping the content fresh. To remain relevant for the kids, approximately six times a year we invite older elementary children to help write the prayers. It's an opportunity to learn what is going on in the lives of our children—what they are seeing and thinking about. The child who helps write the prayer then leads in the prayer time the next Sunday.

While the content is flexible, the weekly ritual is important for both the children and adults. Recently when I was away, another pastor led the children's prayer time. After an excellent prayer, she concluded the time and looked at the children, who looked right back at her. No one moved. My colleague had forgotten to end with the Lord's Prayer, and the children weren't going anywhere. They continue to remind her of this mistake often!

I have been in other congregations that explored many possibilities for engaging the children and their families in worship, including object lessons, children's sermons, and other ideas. Of all the things I have tried, I like this prayer format best. It is rewarding to work with children in worship in this way and to see them grow and learn through a meaningful and memorable ritual.

Examples of Children's Prayer Time

The First Presbyterian Church, New York City, Sunday, May 3, 2009

Children's Prayer

As we gather together today, God, we give you thanks for the many ways that you share with us. On this Sunday we are thinking about the importance of worshiping together and sharing in the Lord's Supper, we think of the importance of gathering together, giving thanks, and remembering all that Jesus taught and did.

We love the feeling of being included. We feel it when we come to church, pray, play with our friends, go on picnics, invite friends over, eat dinner together, play baseball, play chess, and do countless other things. We love the way we feel when we are with our pets and with our families, when we sing together in choir, when we dance and listen to each other. We are glad Jesus included everyone around the table and in the things that he taught. Help us to be thoughtful about how we include others in this week ahead, especially those people and animals who are sick, lonely, and in need of extra care. Bring them the comfort of knowing that you are always with them.

Now let us pray together the prayer that Jesus, our teacher, taught his disciples:

"Our Father . . ."

The First Presbyterian Church, New York City, Sunday, May 10, 2009

Children's Prayer
Let us bow our heads and pray.
Wonderful God, we have learned that to magnify means to make something look bigger. Thank you for our ability, no matter how big, to see how big your love is.
Leader: Our souls magnify you, God,
Response: Our spirits rejoice!

Loving God, we know you have done great things for us.
Leader: Our souls magnify you, God,
Response: Our spirits rejoice!

Great God, we have received so many blessings from you, teach us how to fill the hungry and include those who are often left out.
Leader: Our souls magnify you, God,
Response: Our spirits rejoice!

Merciful God, we remember that your strength and forgiveness are always there for us.
Leader: Our souls magnify you, God,
Response: Our spirits rejoice!

Now let us pray together the prayer that Jesus, our teacher, taught his disciples:

"Our Father . . ."

Ideas to Consider

- How are children included in your worship services now?
- At First Presbyterian, Barbara wants the children to learn the Lord's Prayer. What prayers, recitations, or rituals are most important to your congregation? How could children be included in a significant way?

The Example of a Child

K. C. Ptomey

We did not have children's sermons often in our church, but we did work to include the children in worship. In our young and growing congregation, we had baptisms on the second Sunday of each month. At the beginning of each baptism, we invited all the children to come forward and gather around the baptismal font. Our Director of Children's Education wrote a short vow for the children to repeat in the service: "I will love these babies and teach them about Jesus." The children clearly heard the words and saw the baby anointed with the sign of the cross. It was a wonderful experience.

We always hold a pre-baptism seminar with a time for questions and answers. One evening, a father who was having his fourth child baptized came rushing in late. He was a physician and always was in a hurry. He apologized, and then he told the group that he and his wife had been arguing about who would get to come that night. Frankly, after three baptisms, I hadn't expected to see either of them. But faith formation is a powerful thing. You see, this father wanted to share a story about his four-year-old daughter.

That evening at the dinner table, as the man and his wife discussed the upcoming baptism of the newest addition to the family, one of their preschool daughters got up from her seat and went to the youngest child, who was sitting in an infant chair. She reached down and made the sign of the cross on her brother's forehead. Though she didn't know all the words or the theology, she knew what baptism was about. Her faith is being shaped in a powerful way through her participation in the worship of her church.

III
THE CONGREGATION IN PRAYER

Prayer is crucial to the life of every congregation. Though they sometimes differ in the methods, every congregation should provide for members and visitors a welcoming atmosphere where they can freely receive and offer prayer. Consider the prayer ministry your church currently offers and how it can be renewed and improved. In this section, you will:

- Learn how to create a culture of prayer (or "authentic prayer spaces") in any setting.
- Discover ways congregations can emphasize prayer in the various elements of their life together.
- Receive guidance on leading healing prayers and healing prayer services.
- Consider practical instruction on handling prayer requests, the function of congregational prayer lists, and the use of social media tools (e.g., Facebook, blogging, Twitter) in expanding prayer communities.
- Read helpful outlines for finding and training volunteers in prayer ministry.

Articles:

CREATING SPACE FOR AUTHENTIC LIVING CREATES SPACE FOR AUTHENTIC PRAYER LIVES

Connie and Joseph Shelton

The Rev. Drs. Connie and Joseph Shelton are senior pastors of Galloway Memorial United Methodist Church in Jackson, Mississippi, and previously served as co-directors of Field Education/Church Relations at Duke Divinity School in Durham, North Carolina. In this article, Connie and Joey describe how to create "authentic space" in worship through various avenues of ministry.

The parishioners entered the dimly-lit sanctuary with a sense of anticipation. The acoustic introduction broke the silence and the solo voice began, "When I survey the wondrous cross on which the Prince of Glory died." From hidden places, one by one, congregants walked to the center of the cleared chancel area. Each time one walked front center, she/he held up a piece of cardboard penned with words expressing the pain of life, the ache of sin, or the stress of reality written in raw printed letters. As the onlooking worshippers received the gift of each story, the storyteller flipped over the cardboard to share words . . . words expressing the power of God, the grace of Christ, the sustenance of the Spirit, the strength of communal life. The depth of trust exhibited by those who shared their cardboard struggles was only surpassed by the depth of trust by which the gathered community received the gifts. *(Note: You'll find a Power-Point slideshow of these cardboard confessionals on the accompanying DVD-Rom. See Image Gallery.)*

One is never sure how stories about "drugs and alcohol" or "unplanned pregnancy" might be received. Yet, in the context of authentic worship with authentic sharing, the transformation of the Holy Spirit becomes apparent. Part of the role of worship leadership is recognizing the prayerful connection between presenting needs and the grace of Jesus Christ.

The gift of authentic sharing is surprisingly rare. Sadly, in many congregations, it is easier to "play church" than to "be church." **The beginning of creating authentic prayer lives is creating authentic space in congregations.** It is in the authentic exchange that the power of the God who accepts us "just as I am without one plea" becomes not only real but overwhelms our underwhelmed lives.

What does it mean to live authentically in community? How might authentic living create authentic prayer lives? In 1836, the First Christian congregation of Jackson, Mississippi, was birthed, now known as Galloway Memorial United Methodist Church. Galloway is rich in history and tradition.

Her history is enmeshed with her social location: the Deep South, the Bible Belt, and more particularly, Mississippi and the complexities of the Magnolia State. The complexities of her social location have fostered various opportunities for the congregation to make important communal decisions. During the Civil Rights movement, Galloway's members disagreed about the role of the church within the movement. Their beloved pastor encouraged a policy of racial openness. At a critical juncture, the voices of opposition to racial openness carried the day. The beloved pastor resigned. Later, the voices of open doors prevailed and church policy was reversed. This resulted in the departure of hundreds of parishioners who did not want an open door policy. Those opposed to the open door decision resigned their membership and founded a new independent Methodist church.

In the midst of this turbulence and imbalance, the ethos of seeking grace and following God's will was heightened well beyond business as usual. In spite of the groundwater of broader social conditioning, a watershed moment of deepened authenticity emerged. What passed from this generation of Galloway members to the next is the ability to engage in open dialogue, no matter the cost. The nature of this honest reflection has given the congregation the space to be honest with one other and provided the opportunity for authenticity.

With such a history we should not be surprised by the authenticity of our community. Over and again, people are willing to share the disappointments and celebrations of life. They are open to letting others know of God's continual faithfulness, even when they struggle in their personal and corporate faith journeys. The beauty of authenticity is that it continually surprises us. For that unpredictability of the Holy Spirit's movement, we are grateful.

Prayer is not a program but an ethos. It is in the authentic exchange of/in community that we experience the authentic presence of the Triune God.

Prayer is not a program but an ethos. Congregations form pastors. Pastors form congregations. The Holy Spirit transforms both. It is in the authentic exchange of/in community that we experience the authentic presence of the Triune God. God is certainly not limited to our exchange, but authentic communal life proves to serve as a means of grace.

Prayer is birthed out of authenticity. Being real before God is a practice cultivated. Being real in community is a practice cultivated. The two are intrinsic to each another.

To create an ethos of prayer is to create communal space that is willing to acknowledge individual and corporate reality. It is risky. It is life-giving.

When we make ourselves vulnerable to one another, there is an open door for transformation.

Be clear. Authenticity is *not* "calculated vulnerability" whereby one manipulates another by sharing in order to receive or coerce vulnerability from another. Such tactics create hostage situations and relationships are embedded in fear and exploitation.

Prayer is birthed out of authenticity. Being real before God is a practice cultivated.

Be clear. Authenticity is *not* "boundary-free living" whereby one spills his or her guts with no regard for the recipient of the mess. Such tactics create unhealthy relationships built on guilt and shame.

Authenticity *is* a gift from God whereby people realize they are accepted and loved by the Triune God and the community. It is in that genuine gift we experience the transcendent power of incarnation. Intentionally creating authentic space can arise in all gathered life: through preaching, pastoral prayers, small groups, Sunday school classes, fellowship times, and the intentionality of praying for concerns.

Authentic Space through *Preaching*: We encourage the reading of the Psalms and preach the lectionary Psalms with intentionality. The Psalms teach us to be real by expressing anger, joy, revenge, hope. The balance of honest reflection and expression woven into the message of honest hope in God's transforming power is critical for authentic communal life and personal faith.

Authentic Space through *Pastoral Prayers*: Praying purposive prayers in community gives the worshipper permission to offer to God the fullness of life, joy, and sorrow. We discern themes addressed in the scriptural text and draw those into pastoral prayers. Themes create space for authentic prayer and are helpful for those who may have lost their desire to pray authentically. Through pastoral prayers, we name issues of wellness and want. The issues center on the experiences of the congregation and the global context. Examples of current angst may include: doubt, despair, hatred, infertility, loss, war, ecumenism, fear, emptiness, violence, poverty, anxiety disorders, dis-ease, and financial ruin. Yet God's grace points the worshipping body in the prayerful direction of hope, faith, and love.

Authentic Space through *Prayer Request Cards*: Some congregations create an ethos that alludes, "Leave your concerns and come worship God."

Alternatively, we pray that our ethos is, "Bring your concerns and come worship God." Galloway's worship space invites the worshipper to bring to the pew, kneeling rail, and altar their concerns, pain, disappointment, fear. It is in authentically "showing up" with the stuff of life that we trust God's power to transform all that we are. Prayer Request Cards are located in the pews of the sanctuary. The gathered community shares concerns through the Prayer Request Card. Confidential requests are shared only with the pastoral staff. There is a designation on the Prayer Request Card entitled "I desire a call." Appropriate staff (pastoral or lay) responds to those requests needing personal conversation and care.

Authentic Space through the *Connect Sheet* prayer e-newsletter: The Connect Sheet is a communication tool which shares prayer requests with the community. Recipients of this e-newsletter pray for the concerns listed.

Authentic Space through the care of *Stephen Ministry*: The care shown from Stephen Ministers in the Galloway family is essential to our authentic life together. This confidential ministry provides safe space for persons to share grief, heartache, and frustrations that evolve through life-altering experiences. At present, Galloway has 18 active Stephen Ministers and seven Stephen Leaders.

Authentic Space through a telephone *Prayer Line*: Galloway's 11:00 A.M. Sunday worship service broadcasts live each Sunday on television and the Internet. During the worship service, volunteers answer a "prayer line" and pray with callers. The prayer line remains open to receive requests 24 hours per day, seven days per week, with a voicemail receiver recording the caller's prayer request(s). A prayer line volunteer is trained simply to name the need of the caller against the backdrop of the nature of the Triune God: God is love. Jesus Christ suffers with us and redeems our pain. The Holy Spirit journeys with us and advocates for us.

Authentic Space through a *Prayer Team*: A dedicated group of laity serve as Galloway's prayer team. They receive prayer needs through the **Connect Sheet**, **Prayer Request Cards**, email, website, telephone, and the **Prayer Line**. In various seasons of life, our prayer life may become difficult or even nonexistent. In those critical cycles, we realize the significance of community and the comfort that comes from knowing that others pray for us. When one authentically declares, "I do not have faith to pray"; another in the community humbly responds, "I will pray for you."

Authentic Space through *Staff Prayer* during weekly meetings:
Each week as Galloway's staff gathers, intentional time is spent sharing concerns and praying. The faithfulness of Galloway's staff is grounded in caring for one another, caring for the congregation, and caring for the world. Weekly corporate and private prayer is fundamental to the health of the staff.

Authentic Space through the *Location of the Physical Structure*:
Galloway's physical locale is a memorial to prayer, a monument to prayer, and a living act of how prayer catapults the church into the world. The sanctuary houses a columbarium (a chamber or wall in which urns containing the ashes of the dead are stored). Windows and other articles of the sanctuary are adorned with plaques that remember the communion of saints. The congregation has gathered in the same location since 1839. Architecturally, the facilities are a monument of historic significance. The facilities lie directly between the state capitol building and a city park named Smith Park. The capitol building represents the seat of worldly power for the entire state. People who are homeless frequent Smith Park each day and remind us of the intense poverty that plagues our people. The congregation insists that the church remain physically located between these dichotomies.

Beyond monuments and memorials, the congregation has prayerfully considered how she should be relevant and missionally engaged with the downtown area. This has been no easy task. It has required painful truth-telling and developed over many years. The current result is testimony to authentic prayer. Among other ministries, Galloway houses a superb center for child-care, a respite space for those who are homeless, and a commercial kitchen with a staff and space that welcome nonprofit and governmental functions year-round. In each of these ministry areas, it is the congregation that is blessed. Prayer has been the foundation for the vision and the undergirding means of grace for Galloway's continuation.

The authentic space we have described is a gift from God. The gift is a "means of grace." As John Wesley interprets,

> By "means of grace" I understand outward signs, words, or actions, ordained of God, and appointed for this end, to be the ordinary channels whereby he might convey to men, preventing, justifying, or sanctifying grace.

> I use this expression, means of grace, because I know none better, and because it has been generally used in the Christian church for many ages,—in particular by our own church, which directs us to

bless God both for the means of grace, and hope of glory; and teaches us, that a sacrament is "an outward sign of inward grace, and a means whereby we receive the same." The chief of these means are prayer. . . .[27]

What paralyzes you from a full life? When do you experience disappointment? What gives life meaning? When do you remember feeling most alive? When do you feel most alone? What are the things you're holding too tightly? What or who holds you too tightly? Moving those authentic expressions from community to authenticity with God is the way of a prayerful life.

Summing it all up, friends, I'd say you'll do best by filling your minds and meditating on things true, noble, reputable, **authentic**, compelling, gracious—the best, not the worst; the beautiful, not the ugly; things to praise, not things to curse. Put into practice what you learned from me, what you heard and saw and realized. Do that, and God, who makes everything work together, will work you into his most excellent harmonies. (Philippians 4:8-9, *THE MESSAGE*)

Ideas to Consider

- Consider the questions posed at the end of the article. How can we use the authentic expressions of life to move us into greater authenticity with God through prayer?
- Think of the cardboard confessionals illustrated at the start of the article; what are some ways you can invite and welcome "authentic space" into your congregation?

PRAYING WITH THE SAINTS

Sally Langford

How can older members of a congregation help younger members learn how to pray? The Bible has numerous examples of young believers learning about prayer from longtime members of the faith. The priest Eli explained to the young boy Samuel how to answer when God speaks (1 Samuel 3:1-18). The apostle Paul reminded Timothy how he grew in the faith because of the example of his mother Eunice and his grandmother Lois (2 Timothy 1:5). Paul himself often gave instructions about prayer in his letters to new Christians (Romans 12:12; Ephesians 5:20; Philippians 4:6). And Jesus gave his disciples a prayer to use (Luke 11:1-4), offered advice on persevering in prayer (Luke 11:5-13; 18:1-8), and modeled a life dedicated to prayer (Matthew 4:1-11; 14:23; Mark 14:32-42).

> **The Bible has numerous examples of young believers learning about prayer from longtime members of the faith.**

Longtime, faithful members of the church today can also teach young believers about prayer. In one local church, a homebound member explained to a visiting youth group that prayer was her gift to the faith community. "I can no longer come to church," the woman told the youth. "But I can pray. For that reason, I pray each morning for you and for everybody else at church. Each of you is a beloved child of God!" In another congregation, an older woman now confined to a nursing home described to a visiting church member how a nursing assistant joined her in prayer each evening. "Once I am in bed for the night, she and I pray together. We pray silently or offer our prayers out loud. We always close by praying together the Lord's Prayer."

Seasoned Christians often share their prayer practices spontaneously and without prior planning. But local churches easily can add valuable learning experiences with these Christians to their ongoing ministries with children and youth. In one congregation, a youth Sunday school class prepared a list of adults they identified as "prayer warriors." The youth then visited each of the prayer warriors to hear stories of prayer. Each visit ended with the prayer warrior leading the youth in prayer. In another congregation, each confirmation class member is assigned a prayer partner who is an active member of the church. Throughout confirmation, the confirmands know that they are being lifted in prayer. On Confirmation Sunday, the prayer partners are among those standing with the confirmands. Not surprisingly, the partnership between the confirmand and the praying saint often continues long past the confirmation service.

PRAYING CONGREGATIONS

Sally Langford

Sally Langford *has been a United Methodist pastor for 30 years, serving congregations ranging from very small to very large. She currently serves in Western North Carolina and has co-written books and Bible studies with her husband and fellow pastor, Andy Langford. In this article, Sally offers several examples of ways congregations can emphasize prayer in the different settings and ministries of a church body.*

How does a congregation establish prayer as an indispensable part of its life together? Following a revival, a local church decided to become a praying congregation. Prayer became a major emphasis at worship services, class gatherings, business meetings, fellowship meals, and mission trips. Individuals shared their prayer concerns openly, and people responded with the laying on of hands. Before long, the congregation had experienced a new level of freedom in prayer.

Youth grew to appreciate prayer as much as the adults. On one occasion, the high school youth gathered in the church sanctuary to watch a video celebrating two of that year's graduates. When the video ended, the youth spontaneously gathered to kneel and lay hands on the two graduates. The youth offered prayers of thanksgiving and blessing, and the tears that flowed represented their close relationship with God and one another. As the pastor explained, "There is a growing comfortableness among us with prayer. The more we pray, the more we want to pray. I have jokingly said on a few occasions that if you show up here at church, we're liable to sit you in a chair and pray for you."

No one model of prayer fits each and every congregation. Here are a wide variety of prayer practices in different local churches. Which ones might work in your particular setting?

Prayers in Worship

- Open the worship service with an instrumental piece of music. During the music, the congregation centers itself and prays silently for the particular focus of worship that day.
- Use music throughout the worship service to encourage and focus the prayers of the people. For example, hymns such as "Spirit of the Living God" or "Breathe on Me, Breath of God" can be sung before an opening prayer or pastoral prayer; hymns such as "This Little Light of Mine" or "Lead Me, Lord" might be used in the context of a prayer of commitment or dedication; and hymns such as "Let Us Now Depart in Thy Peace" or "Savior, Like a Shepherd Lead Us" work well during a closing prayer or benediction.

- Invite the congregation to come to the Communion rail to pray during the pastoral prayer or the closing hymn.
- Share prayer concerns from the pulpit, and encourage worshippers to share aloud their own individual prayer concerns.
- Lift up the importance of prayer in sermons. Preach a series of sermons on prayer.
- Worship services may occasionally focus on one specific prayer concern. Pray for a new building program, a stewardship campaign, a particular mission project, or church members in the military. These worship services should include extensive time for silent and spoken prayers, as well as time for singing and reading Scripture.
- Lighted candles enrich a congregation's experience of prayer. Set up a candle stand or votive holder with the needed number of small candles at the front of the sanctuary or worship space. Invite worshippers to light a candle for a person or situation. After their candles are lit, the worshippers can kneel to pray at the Communion rail or return to their seats to pray. Another option is for a leader to read names aloud from a prayer list. As each name is read aloud, family members and friends come forward to light a candle. This is especially appropriate on All Saints Sunday or an Anniversary or Homecoming Sunday. If a candle stand is not available, create a prayer box. Find or construct a wooden box, which is approximately 2 x 3 feet and 5 inches deep. Fill the box with sand and place on a table at the front of the sanctuary. The box may be slightly raised from the rear, in order that the lighted candles may be easily seen.

Spaces and Places for Prayer

- Provide a dedicated space for individual and community prayer. A small chapel is one option, but so is an available classroom, in which an atmosphere of prayer is created through such items as a prayer bench, Bibles, devotional guides, CD player, candles, and comfortable floor cushions and chairs. One congregation leaves a prayer journal on a small desk in the Prayer Room. Individuals write down prayer concerns, which others can read and hold in prayer.
- If a prayer room is not available, create a space for prayer in a highly visible location. Set up a prayer wreath, for example, in the corner of the fellowship hall. Hang various colors of ribbon near the wreath. At their convenience, individuals choose ribbons and then offer prayers, while tying ribbons to the wreath. Bulletin boards or white boards may also be used to list prayer concerns. Pens, note paper, and thumb tacks can be provided, so that individuals might add their own prayer concerns to the board.

Prayer Teams

- Each local church has members who are passionate about prayer. Encourage these members to serve on a prayer team. The prayer team prays for the concerns listed in the bulletin and on the church website, as well as for concerns received through e-mail and at meetings of the church council. When and where the prayer team prays is totally up to team members. The Prayer and Share Group in one congregation meets weekly in the church sanctuary, while another church's Prayer Team gathers on Tuesday evenings at a local restaurant.

- Encourage existing committees and groups to focus on prayer. The Stephen Ministers in one congregation understand that ongoing prayer for the individuals they serve is vital. At another local church, committee chairs and team leaders devote ten minutes of each meeting to prayer.

- Ask a prayer team to pray with the pastor and other worship leaders before worship. At one local church, the prayer team is available in a prayer room for an hour before worship and prays not only for that day's worship service but also with persons desiring intercessory prayer.

Prayer Services and Gatherings

- Invite people to come and pray at the church at specific times during the week. Persons can come and pray with others in the church sanctuary on Wednesday evenings or over donuts in the fellowship hall on Thursday mornings. Find the times and places that best fit the needs of your congregation.

- Establish a gathering for solitude and prayer during a specific season of the year. Invite the congregation to come and pray in the sanctuary one evening each week during the summer months. Instrumental music creates a prayerful atmosphere, while Scripture verses related to prayer are read aloud every twenty minutes. The pastor and lay leaders may be present to pray with those who ask.

- Offer a monthly or quarterly prayer breakfast for the church and community. Include a speaker and music on a topic related to prayer.

- Hold prayer vigils to lift up particular concerns, such as a revival, building campaign, or mission trip.

- Gatherings for prayer are not limited to the church grounds. Invite church members on a Prayer Walk through the neighborhood or community. Pray silently for each house or business while walking. Pray for God's guidance to be the church in ministry to the world.

Ideas to Consider

- Are there any prayer practices listed above that your congregation hasn't tried that might serve the needs of your congregation and community? Which will you adopt?

- Can you think of other physical, tangible means of inviting your members into a practice of prayer?

PRAYER MAKES A DIFFERENCE

Sally Langford

*lly Langford has been
United Methodist pastor
0 years, serving congre-
tions ranging from very
l to very large. She cur-
rently serves in Western
North Carolina and has
written books and Bible
udies with her husband
and fellow pastor, Andy
Langford. In this
icle, Sally describes one
ngregation whose open-
and willingness to pray
s affected both members
and visitors.*

Becoming a praying congregation requires concerted time and effort, but once prayer permeates the congregation, taking time to pray comes easily. In one local
church, volunteer firefighters and first responders are active participants in Sunday morning worship. Occasionally, a house fire or car accident occurs during the worship
service, and the firefighters and first responders are paged
to come quickly. Anytime four or five church members rush
out of worship at the same time, the congregation knows
what is happening. The set order of worship is put aside,
and the congregation prays for the volunteers and the people they are rushing to help.

In a praying congregation, mature, Christlike behavior is demonstrated, too. In this same local church, a visitor showed up in time for Sunday school one Sunday
morning. The visitor stood out in the midst of longtime
members, largely because he was dressed in jogging pants
and bedroom slippers. Even so, several members warmly in-
vited him to come with them to class and afterwards to sit with them in worship.

During the worship service,
the pastor asked the congregation to
share prayer concerns. Hesitantly,
the visitor in the bedroom slippers
raised his hand. The visitor shared
in a quiet voice that he was having

**Becoming a praying congregation
requires concerted time and effort, but
once prayer permeates the congregation, taking time to pray comes easily.**

trouble paying his bills and needed the prayers of the church. During his pastoral prayer, the pastor prayed for the man and asked God to guide the congregation and him in their response to the needs of this newcomer.

Following worship, church members gathered around the visitor for conversation. They discovered that the visitor was new to town; he had recently
lost his job and was living alone. One particular church family, a family of modest means itself, invited the man to come home with them for Sunday dinner.
Family members explained that it was a birthday celebration, but there was always room for one more at the table. After lunch, the man confessed that he

could not remember when he had last had a piece of birthday cake. Other church members responded to the man's needs, as well. Groceries were purchased, as was a new battery for the man's car. It was not long before the man moved on to another town, but the church sent him forth with prayers and with contact information for a new church home.

Prayer made a difference in the life of this congregation. How is prayer making a difference in the life of your local church?

Ideas to Consider

- In the congregation Sally describes, prayer has become an immediate reaction to expressed need. If that is not the case in your congregation, develop a practice of praying for the current needs of your church and community.
- Like the man in the bedroom slippers, are there people in your community and congregation who feel their expressions of needs are welcome? Are their needs being met through prayer and prayerful response?

PRAYER NOTES

Sally Langford

Caring church members often send notes or cards to individuals in need of prayer. One local church found a way to involve the entire congregation in a note-writing ministry. Attractive note cards and envelopes were printed and placed in a basket on a table at the entrance to the church sanctuary. Printed on each card was a flower and the words, "Someone at Central United Methodist Church Sent You A...PETaL!" (Also printed on the card was this explanation of PETaL: **P** for Praise; **E** for Encouragement; **T** for Thanks; and **L** for Love.) Each Sunday morning, church members are encouraged to pick up note cards and write notes to individuals, including those on the prayer list printed in the church bulletin. Completed note cards left on the table will be mailed by the staff on Monday. Church members may also pick up blank note cards and write and mail the notes at their own convenience. The congregation has embraced their "PETaL Ministry," and prayer notes go out into the community every week.

HEALING SERVICES

Andy Langford

...dy Langford, a United ...odist pastor in Western North Carolina, has ...thored several books fo-...g on worship and faith ...d worked extensively on ...United Methodist Hym-...iting the healing work ...Jesus and his disciples, ...y discusses the need for ...rayers for healing and ...ling services in congre-...ations and also offers a ...ggested congregational service of healing.

How do we pray for healing of body, mind, and spirit? The Letter of James offered early Christians instructions about praying together for those persons who need physical, spiritual, emotional, and mental wholeness in their lives:

Is any among you suffering? They should pray. . . . Are any among you sick? They should call for the elders of the church and have them pray over them and anoint them with oil in the name of the Lord. The prayer of faith will save the sick, and the Lord will raise them up; and anyone who has committed sins will be forgiven. Therefore confess your sins to one another, and pray for one another, so that you may be healed. The prayer of the righteous is powerful and effective. (James 5:13-16)

Scripture strongly affirms ministries of healing. The root of the word "healing" in New Testament Greek, *sozo*, is the same as that for salvation and wholeness. Healing in the church is God's work of offering all people balance, harmony, and wholeness of body, mind, spirit, and relationships through confession, forgiveness, and reconciliation. Through such healing, God brings about reconciliation of every kind. Throughout the New Testament, Jesus himself healed the estranged and sick and sent out his disciples on ministries of healing.

Scripture asserts several key affirmations about spiritual healing. All healing is of God. The church's healing ministry in no way detracts from the gifts God gives through medicine and psychotherapy. Healing is not magic, but underlying it is the great mystery of God's love.

A service of healing is not necessarily a service of curing, but provides an atmosphere in which healing can happen. For Christians, the basic purpose of spiritual healing is to strengthen one's relationship with the living Christ.

Those who minister spiritual healing are channels of God's love. God does not promise that we shall be spared suffering, but does promise to be with us in our suffering. God does not promise that we will be cured of all illnesses; we all must face the inevitability of death. A service of healing is not necessarily a service of curing, but provides an atmosphere in which healing can happen. For Christians, the basic purpose of spiritual healing is to strengthen one's relationship with the living Christ.

Prayers for healing may be incorporated into any service of congregational worship as a response to the reading and preaching of the Word. Also, there may be a healing service at a stated time each week or month, or healing may be ministered privately to individuals. Many find that Holy Communion also adds to services of healing.

The additional action of laying on of hands on someone's head or shoulders, and the less formal gesture of holding someone's hand, both show the power of touch and its central role in healing. Jesus often touched others—blessing children, washing feet, healing disease, and raising people from death. Christians also have a natural desire to reach out to persons in need, to touch gently those who ask for healing prayers. Touching is a tangible expression of the presence of the healing Christ, working in and through those who minister in his name. In addition, anointing the forehead with oil is a sign act invoking the healing love of God. The oil points beyond itself and those doing the anointing to the action of the Holy Spirit and the presence of the healing Christ, who is God's Anointed One.

The following is an example of a congregational service of healing:

Gathering
Read James 5:14-16a.

Prayer
Offer a brief prayer for the power of healing.

Scripture
Read one of many biblical lessons about healing, such as Isaiah 35:1-10; Psalm 13; Acts 3:1-10; and Matthew 8:1-13.

Sermon or Meditation
Link the Scripture with the immediate needs of the community.

Confession and Pardon
Allow persons to prepare themselves for healing power through cleansing themselves of sin and guilt.

Holy Communion
The Holy Meal may be served, or not.

Thanksgiving Over the Oil
Bless the gift of oil as a sign of healing.

Prayers for Healing and Wholeness
Persons may kneel, share their need, receive a prayer, have hands laid on them, and be anointed with oil. A prayer might include, "I anoint you with oil in the name of the holy and triune God for healing."

Sharing of Thanksgiving
Persons who feel so led may give thanks for healing or other blessings.

Thirty years ago, a New York congregation opened its doors for a service of healing for persons with AIDS. While many feared AIDS as a new plague and shunned those associated with it, this community of faith offered hospitality, prayer, and human touch to persons suffering. The congregation, in the midst of Greenwich Village, was filled to overflowing every week.

In a North Carolina congregation, one of the pastors was diagnosed with a malignant brain tumor. On her first Sunday back in the congregation following surgery, the children of the church gathered around her, laid hands on her, and prayed for her healing. There were many tears in the sanctuary following the prayer.

In every congregation, there are multiple opportunities for healing services. When persons are grieving the loss of a job or the loss of pregnancy; when persons and their families face mental, physical, and spiritual illness; and especially as persons face death, the congregation can and should pray for healing.

Ideas to Consider

- When might your congregation offer a service of healing?
- Write a service of healing, perhaps following the example offered here.
- What are apparent needs—job scarcity, physical illness, drought—in your congregation and community that your congregation could lift up healing prayer?

CREATING SIGNS OF PRAYER:
Prayer Shawl Ministry

Andy Langford

What are creative ways to use signs and objects to assist in and focus congregational prayer? Throughout the ages, Christians have used religious objects to focus their prayer. During the Middle Ages, cathedrals and other holy sites focused on stained-glass windows and religious relics, including alleged pieces of the cross or the bone of a saint. The famous Shroud of Turin in Italy still attracts pilgrims to see the burial cloth of Jesus. In Avila, Spain, today one may see clothing and even a finger of Saint Teresa.

In modern society, some television preachers advertise small flasks of holy water or a sliver of cloth for prayer. Some congregations distribute "Loving Bears" or fresh, handmade bread, or even quilts as signs of support. And in many churches, people at prayer are invited to light a votive candle to focus their prayers.

In many congregations, a newer tradition has evolved that encompasses the strength of holy objects for communal prayer: prayer shawls. In countless congregations, small clusters of women, and some men, gather in a church parlor or someone's home to knit a shawl or blanket for the sick and other people in need. The groups may be called a "Healing Shawl Ministry" or "Prayer Blanket Partners."

> **In many congregations, a newer tradition has evolved that encompasses the strength of holy objects for communal prayer: prayer shawls.**

These praying partners may gather every week, once a month, or whenever there is a need for more blankets. The yarn may be synthetic or natural, brightly colored or plain, but is almost always soft to the touch. As the metal or wooden knitting needles click, the participants slow down, focus their attention on the task at hand, and share the prayer concerns of their families and friends. More experienced knitters love teaching their skills to new knitters. All these hands become God's hands. As they knit, they describe to one another how they have felt God's healing power in their own lives—recovering from divorce, surviving cancer, and overcoming grief. Everyone speaks and listens as each loop and each knot of each shawl is formed.

At the end of the session, everyone gathers together and lays hands on each completed blanket. They pray over the shawl that the person who receives it will also feel God's power. They offer a prayer of thanksgiving for the ability to use their gifts and a prayer of intercession for the unknown recipient of the gift. Sometimes, all the knitters sign a card of prayer attached to the shawl.

The knitted shawls and blankets are presented to children at their baptism, people who grieve, folks in the hospital, and older persons who are homebound. In one congregation, great-grandmother Helen knits a new baby prayer blanket for every new member of her family. Vicki, with compassion for the sick, makes sure that every person from the congregation who has surgery gets a shawl.

Reta was diagnosed with a malignant brain tumor. Beloved by the women in her congregation, the prayer shawl circle searched through their creations to find the perfect one for her. Multicolored and very soft, the shawl was given to Reta when she returned to her hospital room after surgery. She immediately knew what the gift was, and hugged it to her chest. For the next weeks and months, the shawl remained with her at the hospital, at home, and during her treatments, helping her remember that her friends in Christ were praying for her.

SOCIAL MEDIA AND SPIRITUAL FORMATION:
Using Web-Based Tools to Foster the Prayer Life of a Community

Ben Simpson

Ben Simpson *is a Christian, freelance writer, and school bus driver in his hometown of De Soto, Kansas. Here, Ben examines how various forms of social media can help expand the prayer life of communities and broaden the reach of prayer. He shares his own experience with starting 40 Days of Prayer, a united prayer effort, using social media tools. You can connect with Ben through social media by visiting his website, www.benjaminasimpson.com.*

Prayer is communication with God. We speak, and, if we are wise, we listen. Our witness is at its best when it is grounded in the practice of prayer, and the world of Web-based technology has opened new doors for how we can integrate prayer into our corporate life.

Historically, the prayers of the church have been formed by our worship, through times of private devotion, and in consultation with trusty printed resources. But with recent advances in Web-technology and social media tools, new forms have become available to us that enable us to come together in prayer in new and innovative ways. Twitter, Facebook, blogs, and other social media tools can be used within the contexts of our ministries; and below you will find simple, step-by-step instructions as to how you might use these tools in the prayer life of your community. But first, let me tell you a story.

40 Days of Prayer: The Manifesto

In March of 2009 God took me by surprise. God asked me to call others to pray for The United Methodist Church for a period of forty days. Further, I felt pressed to make that call very specific, in that the form of our prayer would follow the contemplative threefold path of purgation, illumination, and union; that the partners in the effort would be young, emerging leaders within the denomination; and that the content of our prayer would be for people to encounter Jesus Christ through the witness and ministry of United Methodism.

The world of Web-based technology has opened new doors for how we can integrate prayer into our corporate life.

This calling was the outflow of my observation that while the church had done a great deal in terms of casting vision for how we might be about the work of God in the world, there had been too great a silence in calling the church to prayer. My experiences, observations, and passions coalesced as fertile ground where God birthed an idea within me, but considering the fact that I had no formal position of leadership, a limited network, and a foggy idea of the form this invitation would take, the next steps were not immediately clear. I had work to do.

At the time the idea for 40 Days of Prayer for The United Methodist Church first emerged, I had been blogging for a period of a little over one year. I had been involved in the lives and ministries of others across the country through electronic media, and had made a few connections. My wife Molly and I had also established friendships with others in ministry while in seminary, and in the short time she had been serving as a pastor, providing me with names and contact information of a few others with whom I could share my vision.

On the Saturday that this idea congealed, I sat down to compose an email to seventeen of my friends and colleagues in ministry, spelling out clearly the vision for a united prayer effort, while also opening the conversation to others. I did this to widen the possibilities for the scope of the project, knowing that God was moving in the lives of those I contacted. At the conclusion of my email, I let my friends know that I would post my vision to my blog, and that they could pass along the idea "to help me build a movement." You can read the manifesto that started it all at http://bit.ly/pray40.

Over the next six weeks I was astounded by the results. Within two weeks of my initial appeal, I had more than 30 of 40 volunteers needed to write for the campaign. By six weeks, our volunteer list was complete. We had also determined a date to begin the campaign. In concert with Jenny Smith, Andrew Conard, Chris Smith, and Gavin Richardson, work began to launch a young clergy website to host the prayer campaign.

What began as an appeal to a small audience of seventeen and a public declaration on my blog became more than I could've imagined. The compiled project was made available in book form, was utilized by one local church pastor in a weekly radio devotional, and received media coverage from *The United Methodist Reporter*, *Interpreter* magazine, and The General Board of Higher Education and Ministry. The 40 Days campaign began in early May of 2009 and concluded in late June, and took place concurrently with many United Methodist Annual (Regional) Conferences. The campaign was facilitated by the website of the United Methodist Young Clergy network (http://www.umcyoung clergy.com), and included hundreds, if not thousands, of people.

The Ideavirus

So, how did the idea take off? In his book *Unleashing the Ideavirus* (Simon & Schuster, 2002), author Seth Godin argues that ideas spread best when they can be caught like a cold. When an idea "infects" the right people, or is introduced to the right hive, it can take off rapidly in much the same way that the flu spreads through an elementary school. Godin argues that Ideaviruses begin with an idea manifesto, which can be a compactly written essay, a cool image, or a song that creates value and ignites the imagination. The 40 Days of Prayer idea had been captured in electronic form—it was an idea manifesto that could easily be passed on through Web-based media. It was my prayer that we could expose the right people to that idea. If the vision was born of God, it would spur imaginations and fuel a movement of the Holy Spirit.

Andrew Conard, Jenny Smith, and Gavin Richardson are three people who caught wind of the idea early and passed it on to others. Andrew, Jenny, and Gavin had built significant audiences through Twitter, Facebook, and their blogs, and were able to use their influence to help the 40 Days idea take on a definite shape. As they exposed others, their enthusiasm was infectious. Gavin posted a link to my blog post at The Methoblog (http://www.methoblog.com), Jenny began to publicize the idea through the connections she had made with other young clergy, and Andrew publicized the idea on his blog. Through the groundswell on the Web we were able to build our volunteer base, set our agenda, and direct consciousness toward the 40 Days of Prayer campaign.

Expanding Content Delivery

40 Days of Prayer began as an idea manifesto inspired by the Spirit, came to include a number of enthusiastic advocates in Web-space, and was scheduled to take place. Now, we had to unite our participants in prayer. We did this in five ways. Those forms were a blog, an RSS feed, Facebook, Twitter, and a printed booklet. I'll say a brief word about each one.

First, the primary home for the 40 Days of Prayer campaign was a blog hosted by the United Methodist Young Clergy network (http://www.umcyoung clergy.com/prayer). Prayers would be posted to the website daily during the campaign. Anyone who wished to participate could visit the website, click on the appropriate link, and read the prayer for the corresponding day.

Second, the prayer feed made use of RSS (or "Really Simple Syndication") technology. By clicking on the RSS button, users were able to subscribe to the website in a couple of different ways. First, users could subscribe to the website using a Web-based reader, such as Google Reader (www.google.com/reader), Bloglines (www.bloglines.com), or FeedDemon (www.feeddemon.com). Readers allow users to centralize information into one convenient location and update Web content automatically as it evolves. Second, users could subscribe to the website using an RSS feed to their email inbox. When the prayer site was updated, those who signed up to receive notification had new content delivered to their personal email account.

Third, Jenny Smith set up an event for 40 Days of Prayer on Facebook. Facebook (www.facebook.com) is a social networking site where you can connect with "friends" and share information through status updates, notes, pictures, and events. Jenny created an event for 40 Days that was open to all users on Facebook. Participants in the campaign invited their friends to "attend," and

469 people responded that they would take part. Each day Josh Hale, one of the contributors to the 40 Days project, sent daily reminders through Facebook to all confirmed "attendees" with a link to the prayer for each day.

Fourth, Twitter was an important way to communicate and invite others to join us in prayer each day. Participants in the campaign could "tweet," or send a short message to their network with an excerpt from the day's prayer and a link to our website. Word spread when others would "retweet" the original message. A "retweet" (or "RT") repeats the message and gives credit to the originator. Users could also "tag" their messages to show they belonged to the campaign. For 40 Days of Prayer, messages were tagged with #pray40 (on Twitter, a # sign indicates a tag).

Fifth, the written prayers for the 40 Day campaign were compiled into booklet format and published through Lulu.com. Lulu.com is a self-publishing website where you can upload a document, pick out a cover design, and have your written work professionally bound. Knowing that not all persons work best with Web-based forms of communication, we decided that it would be good to put together a printed resource. As a group, contributors to the 40 Days project decided to donate all profits to NothingButNets.net, a nonprofit organization that provides bed nets to combat diseases like malaria among the world's poor. We sold 59 copies (electronic and bound) of the 40 Days guide, raising about $340 for 34 bed nets.

Evaluating the Movement: Friendship, Faithfulness, and Our Future

The 40 Days of Prayer campaign was an unexpected blessing. Through social media, we were able to spread an idea, build a significant base, and bring people together in prayer. Many of the participants in the campaign are now networked together through Facebook, Twitter, and blogs. Conversations that began as part of the 40 Days of Prayer campaign about the future of The United Methodist Church have continued, and many have been dreaming about what God might have for us next. These conversations have served to inspire hope in the denomination, encourage leaders serving in ministry, and spur creativity in local ministry contexts. The good news: Through imagination, vision, and a little willingness to experiment, our story can become your story. You can foster the prayer life of your community through the use of Web-based tools.

What You Can Do: Using Web-Based Media in Your Community

Twitter, Facebook, and connections made through the blogosphere were each important in making 40 Days of Prayer a reality. Using these technologies were people who are passionate about prayer and ministry. 40 Days of Prayer was a comprehensive effort that included people from various parts of the country, but these same tools can be used in local communities to foster connection and prayer for your context. Together we will explore the basics of how each of the tools used in the 40 Days campaign can be utilized in your ministry.

140 Characters to Start a Conversation: Using Twitter

What is Twitter? According to their website, "Twitter is a service for friends, family, and co-workers to communicate and stay connected through the exchange of quick, frequent answers to one simple question: 'What are you doing?' " Twitter allows users to post short, 140-character messages to a Web-based account through an online form or by text message from your mobile phone. Churches and other organizations are using this tool to keep people informed in their ministry, share links to interesting Web-based articles, and stay connected with those in their contexts.

How do I get signed up?

Visit Twitter's website (http://twitter.com) and click the "Get Started—Join!" button to begin the registration process. From there, you will be asked to provide your name and email address; then, you will choose a user name and password for your account. You may want to set up a personal account, or you may want to set up an account for your church or ministry. Once you are set up, you can begin to "Follow" others, and as you make connections others will "Follow" you.

How can I use this tool in my ministry?

Twitter is a communication tool. Your contributions to the Twitterverse (Twitter's wordplay on *universe*) can range from the mundane to the profound. You'll find that people post updates ranging from trips to the grocery store to deep thoughts from theologians and philosophers. Be patient after you get signed up. You'll need time to build your network, connect with others, and find out how Twitter can work best to foster relationships in your ministry. While there are a number of ways Twitter can be used in your ministry, I will mention three.

First, you can inform people of upcoming events in your ministry context. You can share the title of the weekend sermon, the kickoff of Vacation Bible School, or when and where a Bible study will take place. You can also share news of important events in the lives of persons in your congregation (with their permission), such as birthdays, anniversaries, baptisms, or weddings. You can ask people to pray for these happenings.

Second, you can invite those with whom you minister to converse with you on the Web. The Upper Room (http://twitter.com/UpperRoom) invites those in their network to pray for those working for human rights, those in need of Christian friends, or for those facing tragedy, and to "reply with your prayer." To reply, you would enter "@UpperRoom" followed by your prayer. In the same way you can find ways to spur conversation in your ministry context.

Third, you can pass along information found on the Web. If you post an article to a blog or have an extended update on your ministry website, you can pass along the link on Twitter. If the link is long, utilize TinyURL (http://tinyurl.com) or bit.ly (http://bit.ly) to shorten the entry and keep your post under the 140-character limit. Each day during the 40 Day campaign, participants put a link to the UMC Young Clergy prayer page.

For an example of a church and an individual using Twitter in their ministries, check out Trinity UMC in Lafayette, Indiana (http://twitter.com/TrinityUMCLaf), or Josh Hale (http://twitter.com/expatminister), the Wesley campus minister at Lamar University in Beaumont, Texas.

What creative ways can Twitter foster prayer in a congregation?

In addition to allowing users to check in on their network via the Internet, Twitter can also be synced with a mobile device. You can set Twitter to send messages from designated accounts directly to your phone. Under "Settings" on your Twitter homepage, click "Devices," then follow the instructions to activate updates to your phone. You can instruct those in your ministry how to set up a Twitter account and how to activate mobile updates to stay up to the moment on what is happening in the life of your ministry.

Mobile updates could be used to remind people to pray with and for one another during a particular season of the liturgical year. For example, leaders in your community could band together to compose an online devotional guide for Advent. Once the content is posted online, a reminder to check it out could be sent via Twitter to those who choose to receive your updates on their mobile device.

Another way to use mobile updates: use Twitter to invite others to pray the hours. In the morning, at midday, and in the evening you can schedule Twitter updates to issue the call to prayer, making the modern-day text message alert reassemble the ancient sound of the cathedral bells. You can schedule these updates ahead of time using services such as TweetLater (www.tweetlater.com) and Twuffer (twuffer.com), and the call to prayer will issue forth automatically from your account.

Connecting With Friends: Facebook

Facebook (www.facebook.com) is the world's largest and most active social networking site. According to Facebook's site statistics, their site has 200 million active users worldwide, with 100 million users accessing their accounts daily. After creating an account you are able to connect with friends and share information with others through status updates, photo and video uploads, notes, and by information on your profile. With Facebook you can set up a group or fan page that can connect those in your ministry, enabling you to share news, prayers requests, or words of encouragement with your network.

How do I get signed up?

To sign up for Facebook, visit their website (www.facebook.com) and look for the "Sign Up" form. Facebook will ask for your name, your email address, your gender, your birthdate, and a password. Once you have entered that information, you will be sent to your new profile page, where you can begin to fill in information about yourself, including favorite music, books, movies, television shows, quotations, and hobbies. You can also include your educational background, your hometown, and other general information. Once you have set up your account, you can begin searching for friends, send "friend requests," and build your network. If you need help, Facebook is used by people of all ages, so you should have no trouble finding others who can help you get connected.

How can I use this tool in my ministry?

Facebook is an open channel for communication between people. You'll be amazed at what people contribute to the site in the form of short status updates, longer notes, or pictures and images from daily life. Through Facebook I have learned about life events from new births to sudden losses and deaths, and as a result have been able to respond quickly to friends as their life unfolds with a phone call or by sending an electronic or handwritten note.

Staying up-to-date with your friends on Facebook can help you be in tune with what is happening in the life of those you lead in unexpected ways. Teenagers, in particular, are very transparent with their lives in Web space. Facebook can inform how you pray with and for your people.

What creative ways can Facebook foster prayer in a congregation?

There a number of creative ways Facebook can be used to foster prayer in a congregation. Here are three: (1) creating a Facebook group; (2) creating a fan page; and (3) creating an event. Let's look at how you can accomplish each one.

First, you can create a group for your ministry. Once you have set up your Facebook account, visit http://www.facebook.com/grouphome.php and click "Create a New Group." Once you have provided information about your group you can invite others in your network to join. From the group homepage you can send messages to members, start discussions using the Discussion Board, or upload pictures and videos from ministry events. Group pages provide a number of different opportunities to start conversations, to discover prayer needs, and to share prayer requests with group members.

Second, you can create a fan page for your organization. To create a fan page visit http://www.facebook.com/pages/create.php and follow the instructions. Once your page is set up you can invite others to become "fans." Fan pages are different from group pages in that you can subscribe using SMS, or "Short Messaging Services." The "Subscribe Via SMS" button is located on the lefthand side of the fan page in the menu bar. When you subscribe, fan page updates are sent directly to your mobile phone.

Third, you can create events for your ministry on Facebook and invite others to attend. Once you have set up your account visit http://www.face book.com/events.php and click "Create an Event." For 40 Days of Prayer, Jenny Smith created an event that was open to all of Facebook. Everyone who accessed the event could easily pass on the invitation. For those who "attended," a reminder was placed in the righthand column of their feed each day, and daily messages were sent by an administrator providing the link to that day's prayer. The Facebook event feature could be used as a reminder for sustained periods of prayer or devotion during Lent, Advent, a stewardship campaign, or other special event in the life of your ministry.

Starting a Blog and Using RSS

Blogs are like an online journal where a wide variety of information can be made available, such as news, video, photography, and interesting links. Blogger (www.blogger.com), Wordpress (www.wordpress.com), and TypePad (www.typepad.com) are three prominent blogging websites that you can utilize for free. Blogs allow readers to interact with your content by leaving comments or by linking back to your webpage, creating a form of online conversation.

How do I get signed up?

To sign up for a blog you will first need to choose a blogging platform. I have mentioned three, but other services do exist. After researching your options and choosing a platform, follow the instructions provided by the blogging service and set up your site. Once you have your blog set up, you can use it to generate written prayers, pass along devotional material, or pass along news about what is happening in your ministry.

How can I use this tool in my ministry?

People use blogs in many different ways. To cite one example, Church of the Resurrection in Leawood, Kansas, uses a blog site to supplement their daily devotional guide (GPS—Grow. Pray. Study.) at http://gpsinsights.wordpress.com. Church members can visit the website to read reflections on the devotional readings.

In the 40 Days of Prayer campaign, our team used a blog to publish the prayers from our contributors. Our website enabled us to schedule these posts ahead of time. In your ministry you could do the same. You could gather together a team of creative people in your congregation to write prayers during a particular season of life in your ministry, collect their written materials, publish them to a blog, and encourage your people to visit the blog each day to pray a prayer along with the congregation.

Most blogging websites will feature an RSS ("Really Simple Syndication") button which you can add to your page. Enabling RSS allows users to subscribe to your blog through a reader or by receiving updated content in their email inbox. Feed readers and email inboxes both have functions that allow users to forward your content on to their friends as well, making your prayers, news, and updates easy to pass along.

What creative ways can my blog foster prayer in a congregation?

Use your imagination. Through blogging you can establish a network, make written prayers public, invite others to participate in liturgy, and bring others together in a common life. Generate quality content, invite others to participate, and build an online community of prayer.

Self-Publishing

Electronic media is great and can be used to coordinate a largescale prayer campaign or to quickly inform your network of present prayer needs. But print resources are still valuable and can further your impact. Lulu.com is an online website that will publish your work. You can have a written prayer guide printed and bound, or you can make your collection available as an eBook. Visit Lulu.com, check out their products and services, and see if the resources there could further your ministry.

Tools Change: Stay Savvy

The Web is constantly evolving. Web tools like Facebook and Twitter have been labeled Web 2.0 technologies. That means Web 3.0 is just around the corner. It is only a matter of time before someone conceives of a high-quality, user-friendly Web-based tool that will change the landscape of the Internet. Stay up to date. Ask teenagers what they are using, and why. And then start dreaming. Ask yourself, "How could this be used for ministry?" Then, get to work. Generate helpful content that is deeply rooted in the life you live with God, and invite others to join with you.

Web-based tools provide us one more way to live life with God together. Get creative. You can do it.

Ideas to Consider

- Think about how starting a prayer blog or Facebook page might help your congregation broaden the scope of prayer in your community. What age groups could you reach? What events could you plan?
- Ben offers many suggestions for how to further ministry online; he mentions several ongoing ministries that are actively using social media tools. Visit some of the sites and get inspired!

TRAINING PRAYER MINISTRY VOLUNTEERS IN THE LOCAL CHURCH

Laurie Lowe Barnes

Laurie Lowe Barnes *is pastor of Bristol Hill United Methodist Church in Kansas City, Kansas. Previously she served as Pastor of Prayer and Congregational Care at The United Methodist Church of the Resurrection in Leawood, Kansas. Here, Laurie briefly outlines the biblical call to prayer for others, followed by practical suggestions for training volunteers in intercessory prayer, healing prayer, and in praying one-on-one with individuals.*

Outline for the Training:

God's Calling to Prayer Ministry

Intercessory Prayer – Praying for submitted prayer requests

Healing Prayer – Praying in the hospital can include such times/places as:

- Pre-surgery/procedure
- Serving as a praying presence with friends/relatives in the waiting room
- Post-surgery/hospitalization
- Prayer for the dying and their loved ones

The prayers you offer in the hospital will depend on the situation.

Praying One-on-One – Praying for congregants in a prayer chapel or at the altar during or after a worship service

---

The success of a prayer ministry is formed by finding people who feel called to this service and offering them encouragement, training, and support. Here, I outline the training that I have used in my own congregations, focusing on three areas of prayer ministry—responding to requests, visiting those who are ill or homebound, and prayer support in and after worship.

God's Calling to Prayer Ministry

A) Jesus expects us to pray (Matthew 6:5). The usage of the word "whenever" in this passage from the Sermon on the Mount makes it clear that prayer is not optional for disciples but, rather, is expected.

B) As disciples of Jesus Christ, we are commanded to love God with all our heart, soul, mind, and strength and to love our neighbor as ourselves. In Mark 12:29-31, Jesus calls these the two greatest commandments.

C) Through prayer, we can both communicate with God and love our neighbor as ourselves. Lifting up the needs of our neighbor(s) to God is one of the most basic and important aspects of prayer ministry in the local church.

D) In the local church, there will be many ways that we can live out our calling to prayer ministry. Three of these ways are:

- **Responding to written prayer requests.** Written prayer requests need to be responded to with timely prayer and with a handwritten note to the one who submitted the prayer request. The prayer ministry volunteer should keep the person/situation in their prayers for at least one week. Depending on the way the prayer request card/Web request is designed, the individual submitting the prayer request may ask for a call from a pastor as well. Prayer requests received in weekend worship should be responded to as promptly as possible—by Tuesday of the following week if at all possible.

- **Visiting those who are hospitalized or homebound** and praying with/for them (see "Healing Prayer").

- **Praying for those who are leading and attending the worship services.** Some churches have teams of people who pray for the worship services either before or during those services. They will pray for those who are leading the service (pastors, liturgists, musicians, acolytes, and so forth) as well as those who are attending the service. If your church does not have such a team, mobilize all of the prayer ministry volunteers to be the **Worship Prayer Team** while they attend worship. Challenge them to look around before and during the service and observe and pray for those sitting around them. In addition, some churches will have teams of people pray over the seats/pews in the sanctuary before worship services. This is especially meaningful before services, such as Christmas Eve and Easter, when many who don't regularly attend worship services will be present.

Intercessory Prayer

A) Ask a volunteer to read Exodus 17:8-13 and Colossians 4:2-4 aloud for the group. (Encourage the reader to pronounce any challenging words with confidence. Chances are that no one else in the group will know the correct pronunciation for tough geographical names such as "Rephidim" either!) After each passage, ask the group, "What do we learn about intercessory prayer from this passage?"

B) Ways to manage prayer requests. There are times when we can feel overwhelmed by the needs of the people in our congregation. Here are some suggestions for organizing prayer requests:

1. Make a **Top Ten list** and update it weekly.
2. Organize prayer requests by **days of the week**. A sample weekly list might be:
- Monday – pray for those hospitalized in your church
- Tuesday – pray for those who are homebound
- Wednesday – pray for those who are unemployed
- Thursday – pray for those who are grieving
- Friday – pray for any who are imprisoned—either incarcerated or imprisoned by addiction or fear
- Saturday – pray for those who will be leading the weekend worship service(s)
3. Ask the prayer ministry volunteers for their suggestions as to how best to organize prayer requests. Someone in your group will probably have a great method that we haven't thought of!

C) Prayer was a vital part of the Methodist movement as led by John and Charles Wesley. Discuss John Wesley's statement, "God moves in response to prayer"[28] with the group.

Healing Prayer

A) Ask a volunteer to read Ecclesiastes 3:1-8. What can we learn about healing prayer from this passage?

B) In General:
1. Pray in the car/parking lot before entering the hospital. Ask the group, "What are some things one could pray?"
2. When praying at the bedside, a good initial question to ask is "How are you feeling?" Touch the hand of the person if possible/permissible. Don't interrupt while they are sharing what is going on with them. Your major function during the visit may be simply to be present and perhaps weep with the person.
3. Conversation involves both speaking and listening. Be an observant visitor and take your cues from either the hospitalized person or the family member(s) in attendance. Remember what you hear and use the words of the person or their family in your prayer.
4. Be sure to ask the hospitalized person if it is okay for you to pray for them. It is ok if they say no. If they say yes, consider including everyone in the room and hold hands in a circle. Again, it is ok if some family/

friends choose not to participate. Usually, however, such prayer seems to be a blessing to all who are in attendance.

5. In your prayer, remember to keep a balance between hope and reality (especially for the terminally ill). Death can also be a way of God putting his healing touch on someone. Praying for healing is always appropriate provided one does not dictate to God how/when that healing should occur.

C) Two misconceptions about healing prayer are:

1. We've all heard well-meaning individuals exhort those who need healing, "You have to have enough faith." The type of faith that leads to healing is not a form of positive thinking but, instead, it is the receiving of a good gift that comes from God.

2. Sometimes people are reluctant to pray because they feel that they don't know the "right" way to pray or that they don't know the "right" words to say. Healing prayer is not a question of saying the "right" words as if they were a magical formula. There are some prayer practices that are helpful and scripturally based such as praying in Jesus' name (Acts 3:6, 16), anointing with oil (James 5:14), and the practice of laying on of hands (Acts 28:8). But healing does not depend on strict observance to such practices.

D) "Healing is a gift that can come through prayer, but as a gift it is not something we can control."[29] Do you agree? Why or why not?

Praying One-on-One
(especially in a prayer chapel or at the altar in worship)

Depending on your church, there may be opportunities every week to pray with other members or attendees. Your church may have a prayer chapel or room where people can go either to have times of quiet prayer or ask for someone to pray with them. There may also be times of prayer offered in the sanctuary as a part of the worship service. These kinds of one-on-one opportunities can have elements of both intercessory prayer and healing depending on the circumstances of the individual requesting prayer. Some suggestions for this kind of one-to-one prayer are:

A) When approaching someone in a prayer chapel or at the altar, trust your judgment and the prompting of the Holy Spirit.

B) Ask, "Would you like someone to pray with you?" Ask the group for other suggestions that they have used when initiating prayer with someone.

C) It's ok if they say no. Many people are private individuals and do not feel comfortable sharing what is uppermost on their hearts and minds. Respect that.

D) Whether or not the person lets you pray with them, encourage filling out a prayer request card. That will serve as a visual reminder to you to keep that person in your prayers.

E) Discuss the following statement by John Bunyan: "In prayer it is better to have a heart without words than words without a heart."[30] Do you agree? Why or why not?

Closing

Go around the room and ask people to share, as they feel led, at least one "keeper" about prayer ministry that they will take with them. Such a summary done by the participants is often more effective than the leader's summarization.

Close the training time with a prayer such as the following:

"Thank you, Lord, for giving me the opportunity to serve you through serving others. Through the blessing of your Holy Spirit, make me both equal to the task and worthy of it."[31]

— Tracy Macon Sumner

Ideas to Consider

- Does your congregation currently have a Prayer Ministry through which volunteers are trained and practice prayer? If not, consider arranging an informational meeting for interested members. Cover together the key components of healing, intercessory, and one-on-one prayer that Laurie outlines here.
- If your congregation does have a Prayer Ministry, how do you train new volunteers and renew the training of "seasoned" team members?

HANDLING PRAYER REQUESTS

Kim Thomas

Kim Thomas, *with her husband, Jim, pastors The Village Chapel in Nashville, Tennessee. She is also a painter and a published author. Here, Kim describes how her congregation chose an "old school" approach in a new form to handle prayer requests.*

Our attempts at incorporating prayer into the life of The Village Chapel were not instant fits. But eventually, we resorted to an "old school" approach for our prayer ministry: we began a prayer chain. I must say that I believe that was where the heart first beat in our church's prayer experience. Many years before, there were telephone prayer chains, and mimeographed handout prayer lists. Lists were mailed or distributed at Sunday services, and emergencies were prayed over by well-managed and organized strings of phone calls. It was a sort of sacred version of the children's game of cans and strings, a connection that enabled them to communicate at a distance. So while these old forms served the church so beautifully in a particular season, the new form we did choose to use was email.

We began a simple clipboard sign-up system, passing it around at various gatherings for people to sign up. Weekly, concerns would circulate via the "cans and strings," and hearts would unite over needs and praises. The timeliness of this technology is perfect for prayer teams, and I particularly love it because the list stays before my eyes each week by being in my inbox. The next week, I scoop the previous week's email into a specific "Prayer" mailbox, and store it for future reference and encouragement at the end of the year.

We have a faithful woman at our church who volunteered to manage this early on, and now, several years later, she still quietly, lovingly tends it behind the scenes every week. My guess is that most hurting and anxious ones who send in requests to our prayer list don't know her face, but they know her ministry. She responds to the requests that come in herself, nurturing and caring for the person behind the email, and then collects the week's needs and forwards them to those who have signed up to receive the prayer list. She always begins the list with a reminder to pray for something in the life of our church at large, then lists the needs and the name and email of the person who sent it in (so those receiving the list can also send notes of encouragement, email prayers, offers to help or serve), and closes with a Scripture of encouragement.

At first, she would simply send the requests as they were received. But it wasn't long before the requests came so frequently that we decided to limit it to a weekly email, and we now place a gentle and loving reminder that we would love to join people in praying, and that they should have their requests in by Tuesday for the Wednesday email. Of course, as emergencies arise, we send out those emails, but for the most part, we simply send the weekly list. I thank God that He is not bound by linear *chronos* time, but instead lives and acts in *kairos* time, a more all, then, and now sense of time. If I pray today about something that was needed yesterday, God hears me when the need was greatest, not in the limited time we function here in the fallen creation.

As time and technology have progressed, we are availing ourselves of more new forms. Our website offers a link for sending prayer requests, and we have a place on the website for people to sign up to receive the weekly prayer list. Replacing clipboards and paper with computer and email seems to be another new form we have adapted to easily.

I pray more faithfully with these reminders, and I enter the community more easily because I know the needs more intimately.

It's difficult to describe this process in beautiful terms and words, imbuing it with the appropriate sacredness. But I can honestly say that there is a physical pause I feel when I open mail on my computer and see an email from "Prayer@thevillagechapel.com." I pray more faithfully with these reminders, and I enter the community more easily because I know the needs more intimately.

Sacred emails, blessed stories of thanksgiving, of aches and sufferings, collections of the broken and the lost, the willing and the interceded for, the known and the unknown, have been at the foundation of building our corporate prayer experience at The Village Chapel.

Ideas to Consider

- How does your congregation handle prayer requests?
- Think of Kim's assessment that she enters the church community more easily because she knows the needs of the people more intimately. Do you share this feeling of ease and intimacy with your congregation because you know their prayer needs?
- For another approach to receiving prayer requests, see the accompanying DVD-Rom. There, you'll find examples of prayer request cards provided by Galloway Memorial United Methodist Church. (See Image Gallery.)

CONGREGATIONAL PRAYER LISTS

Andy Langford

How can your congregation involve everyone in praying for all the needs within a congregation? One simple way is to establish and maintain a prayer list for the whole congregation. A prayer list should contain the needs of particular members of the congregation; the names of friends and families with specific concerns; leaders of the nations; the millions of people battling disease, poverty, and war; and the concerns of all creation. Sometimes the list contains only names; some congregations include the names of every person in the congregation. At other times, the list includes a brief statement about the needs: illness, divorce, job loss, or grief. Be careful, however, to honor confidentiality; not everyone wants the whole community to know their specific needs. Prayer lists are an excellent means for stretching the awareness of the congregation of the needs of others, both in their own community and around the world.

Christians have discovered all kinds of ways to maintain such prayer lists. Some congregations keep the list on their website. Others post the list in public areas around the church. Copies are often taken and added to individual prayer notebooks. Others keep the lists on personal computers or PDAs so that they can easily add and delete names. Similar to Roman Catholic rosaries,

Prayer lists are a great way to jog our memories about those . . . in need and to keep [us] returning to God in prayer.

prayer beads, with each bead representing an important person, work for others at prayer (see article on page 156). Whatever form a congregation chooses, prayer lists are a great way to jog our memories about those people and situations in need and to keep the whole community returning to God in prayer.

Dr. James Powell, the senior pastor of several major congregations in North Carolina in the middle of the twentieth century, believed strongly in the efficacy of a prayer list. For the first hour of every day, he prayed through the membership list of the church. On some days Dr. Powell covered a hundred names; other days he focused on a few people in deep need. Dr. Powell's congregation knew not to interrupt him during this hour. And church members gave thanks that Dr. Powell was lifting their names to God.

Prayer lists can take on added significance during particular seasons or events during the year. Pray, for example, for youth and their leaders before a youth mission trip. Or before a revival or stewardship campaign, or during Advent or Lent, ask the congregation to pray for one another by name. If the congregation is facing a pastoral transition or is immersed in serious conflict, then ask members to pray for one another. Prayer lists can change the spiritual environment of the whole church.

IV.

TEACHING PRAYER PRACTICES WITH CHILDREN, YOUTH, AND ADULTS

It is through prayer that we communicate with God and grow in our relationship with God. Prayer is essential to spiritual growth. This is why one of the most important roles of the church is to teach and encourage a life of prayer for all ages. Providing a variety of prayer practices for different age groups and personality types ensures that everyone receives the instruction and encouragement he or she needs. As you reflect on the prayer practices of your church, you and your team will:

• Review and outline the focus of prayer instruction in your church.
• Look carefully at the ways you currently help different age groups develop a relationship with God through prayer.
• Consider how are you encouraging teens to find authentic ways of praying.
• Explore the kinds of creative prayer tools are you using with children, youth, and adults.
• Think through the variety of prayer forms and experiences your church offers and consider their appeal to both introverts and extroverts.

PRAYER AND CHILDREN

Leanne Ciampa Hadley

Leanne Ciampa Hadley, president and founder of the First Steps Spirituality Center* and United Methodist pastor, suggests that our responsibility is not to teach children to pray but to provide four things that will encourage and support them in developing their own relationship with God.

The LORD called Samuel again, a third time. And he got up and went to Eli and said, "Here I am, for you called me." Then Eli perceived that the LORD was calling the boy. Therefore Eli said to Samuel, "Go, lie down; and if God calls you, you shall say, 'Speak, LORD, for your servant is listening.'" So Samuel went and lay down in his place. Now the LORD came and stood there, calling as before, "Samuel! Samuel!" And Samuel said, "Speak, for your servant is listening." (1 Samuel 3:8-10)

This story is my favorite scriptural example of how we as religious leaders, parents, grandparents, Sunday school teachers, and other influential adults can teach children about prayer. In this story, Samuel is still a child and is sleeping when God speaks to him. He does not recognize the voice of God and believes that Eli, the temple priest he lives with, is calling him. At first, Eli has no idea what is going on, but after God calls the third time, Eli recognizes that it is God who is calling the boy. So he instructs Samuel to lie back down (be still), speak to God, and listen to what God has to say.

Notice that in this story, Eli believes the boy Samuel is able to hear and speak to God, and he allows Samuel to have his own relationship with God. Eli does not jump up, interpret what God is saying, and then tell Samuel about it. Rather, Eli gives Samuel the space and responsibility to speak and hear God on his own. Later, Eli hears what God has spoken, and it is not good news for him. Still, he trusts that Samuel had a real encounter with God and listens with respect to what Samuel has heard.

God still speaks today to all of us, including children! Many times we have a hard time believing that it is God who is calling and an even harder time being still and listening. As the adults who guide children toward a spiritual life with God, it is our responsibility—and our blessing—to do for children what Eli did for Samuel so that they can learn as early as possible to listen and speak to

* The First Steps Spirituality Center is dedicated to providing spiritual support to hurting children and teens and educational tools and events for adults wanting to learn about the spirituality of children. For more information, visit www.1ststeps.net.

God. In this precious relationship, they will grow spiritually as God feeds their spirits.

Children have their own relationship with God . . . God will speak to them just as God speaks to us.

One of the reasons we find it difficult to teach children to pray is that we believe we must do the work. I believe that, like Samuel, children have their own relationship with God, and that God will speak to them just as God speaks to us on a daily basis. Our task, then, is not to teach children to pray; it is to provide for them the four things that Eli provided for Samuel:

1. He helped the child to be still.
2. He told him to speak to God.
3. He encouraged him to listen to God.
4. He respected that Samuel had heard God's voice.

1. Help Them to Be Still

First, we must help children to be still. Being still is not a natural thing for children. They are in constant motion, and their minds are stimulated by everything around them. Being still is not "making them" sit like soldiers at attention but creating spaces, both physically and emotionally, where children can focus on God's presence.

Creating a sacred space includes turning off the television, putting toys out of sight, and creating a holy space that interests children and invites them to prayer. A sacred space might be a special table with prayer tools that are brought out only for prayer time. It might be a special blanket spread on the ground for the child to sit on during prayer time, or a special box containing spiritually significant objects or symbols that is opened only during prayer time. You also might create a sacred space simply by turning off the lights and lighting an electric candle. The reason for creating a physical prayer space is to help children begin to focus on the importance of prayer time and to create an atmosphere of quiet and stillness without demanding that children be still.

Being still is . . . creating spaces, both physically and emotionally, where children can focus on God's presence.

A ritual that is attached to the prayer space can help children to quiet down and focus. For example, you might sing a hymn or lullaby or sit on the edge of the bed and cuddle while they relax and prepare to pray. The way we approach the sacred space is also important. Our actions, as well as our words, should demonstrate that this is a holy prayer time. The space needs to be set up calmly and with great intention. As we model the importance of the sacred space, we help children ready themselves for prayer.

2. Teach Them to Speak to God

Eli invited Samuel into the sacred space by having him lie down and be still. Then he invited the child to speak to God. Eli told Samuel what he might say. As the adults in children's lives, we can do the same, but we must remember that words are not the primary way children communicate. Although word prayers such as bedtime and meal prayers are important to include in a child's prayer life, they are not the only way children can be encouraged to communicate with God.

I like to use "prayer tools" with children. Prayer tools are tangible items children can touch and hold that help them to put into symbols, words, and pictures the things they need to say to God. They include things such as clay, paper and crayons, sandboxes, pipe cleaners, and musical instruments. Prayer time might be playing music and allowing children to dance with a streamer; or it might be helping them make a motion, such as a cross or heart, using their whole body to connect with God during prayer. Children often lack the verbal skills to create sentences and prayers as adults do. Instead they can communicate with God by drawing a beautiful rainbow, making an animal out of clay, or experiencing stillness as they stick their hands in sand or water. Many times creative methods of prayer such as these may not look like prayer, but we, like Eli, must trust that children have their own relationship with God and that, in the stillness, God will speak to them.

> **Prayer tools are tangible items children can touch and hold that help them to put into symbols, words, and pictures the things they need to say to God.**

3. Encourage Them to Listen to God

Prayer tools not only equip children to focus on God, they also enable them to communicate with God in age-appropriate ways that extend the time they ordinarily might spend praying and listening to God. For example, if you asked a third grader to pray with words for her grandmother who is ill, she most likely would say something such as, "Dear God, help Grandma get better. Amen." This would take about five seconds. However, if you asked the same child to draw a picture of the same prayer, she might spend five or ten minutes in prayer, opening up space for listening.

Similarly, if you asked a child to be in God's presence by sitting still, he might be able to sit for thirty seconds before becoming distracted. However, if you gave him a lap harp to play, he might spend five to ten minutes creating a beautiful song of prayer that becomes a vehicle for expressing his thoughts and feelings as well as for experiencing God.

For children who are unsure of what they need, such as children who have lost a parent or whose father or mother has been deployed for military service, a prayer tool such as a sandbox gives them space to be still and simply be in the presence of God. Before long they will begin to draw symbols such as peace signs, hearts, and rainbows in the sand, discovering a way to express their feelings to God and be open to God's response.

Prayer tools encourage children to be still, to communicate with God, and to listen. In this intentional, holy time, a sacred space is created in which God can speak clearly to them. This communication might be in the form of words or thoughts, as God spoke to Samuel, or it simply might be an experience of the love of God and the awareness that God is working in their souls.

4. Respect Their Experience as Authentic

After Samuel spoke and listened to God, Eli asked him what God had said and believed what the boy told him. After children pray, it is important to ask if God spoke to them and what they felt. This can be tricky, because we don't want to shame a child who felt nothing or who cannot find words to express what happened to him or her in prayer. Even so, simply asking these questions helps children to understand that prayer is not something we do but something we experience. Something should happen in prayer. We might experience a sense of peace, we might hear God speak, or we might discover clarity to a problem we have been struggling with. Asking children if they experienced anything allows them the opportunity to share. Then, when they share, we must respect and accept their experience as authentic, just as Eli did for Samuel.

> **If we ask children to share, and then question or doubt what they have said, they soon will learn to doubt their own spirit and stop listening to God. When we hear and believe them . . . they will continue exploring prayer and its power.**

Accepting a child's experience as authentic is not as easy as it sounds. We have been conditioned to doubt within ourselves whether or not God has spoken to us. Discernment is difficult for us, and so we doubt what a child experiences, believing they are too young or too naive to truly know if God was present or what God said. If we ask children to share, and then question or doubt what they have said, they soon will learn to doubt their own spirit and stop listening to God. When we hear and believe them, on the other hand, they will continue exploring prayer and its power.

Another reason it may be difficult to hear what children say is because often it is "cute." We laugh at what they say because it is endearing, but they can easily interpret our giggles as making fun of them or thinking they are stupid. It is better to use our words and tell them that what they have said warms our heart and makes us smile than to simply laugh.

The Greatest Gift We Can Give

We, like Eli, must trust that children are capable of having a relationship with God and help them to identify and strengthen that relationship by assisting them in discovering the power of prayer. We can do this by helping them be to be still, giving them tools to speak to God, encouraging them to listen to God, and affirming that they have indeed experienced God in prayer. In these ways we will help children to discover the Rock that they can stand upon for the rest of their lives. It is the greatest gift we can give to them!

One of my dearest friends was dying of cancer. She was a single mom of a second grader. While she was in the hospital, her son lived with my family. Each night, her son and I would go into the guest room, where he slept, and pray. One night he used clay to make a huge cross on top of a hospital bed, and he asked God to watch over his mom and be close to her. Another night he drew a picture of his mother painting a picture (she was an artist).

I had placed a photo of his mom next to the lamp on the table beside his bed. One night he turned this lamp on and off repeatedly. I asked him why he was playing and not saying his prayers. He turned to me and said, "I am praying. This light is the light of God, and I am asking it to shine on mom and heal her." He turned the light on and off several more times and then turned it off and went to sleep. Night after night, he turned the light on and off as his prayer before falling asleep.

The night his mother died, he crawled into bed and turned the light on and off several times. Then he said to me, "Leanne, I am going to leave the light on tonight, okay?" I said, "Sure, are you scared of the dark tonight?" He said, "No, if I wake up, I want to remember that my mom lives in God's light forever now!"

I did not teach this child that his mom lived in God's light. I did not have words to comfort him the night his mom died. It was in this time of sacred prayer, which too many adults would have looked like playing, that God was able to remind this child of God's light and presence at all times, even death. All I did was allow him the space to speak to God in his childlike way so that he might hear and experience God for himself.

Recently, while I was teaching the four- and five-year-old Sunday school class at our church, we spent time in contemplative prayer. I placed yeast in a bowl of warm water and told the children that when we calm our hearts and minds, we can sometimes feel God's love bubble up inside us, much like the yeast was bubbling in the stillness of the water. We practiced being very still and listening for God. After we finished, a five-year-old boy turned to me and said, "I felt God! It was like I had the whole world inside my heart!"

When we encourage and support children in prayer, we become for them an Eli and they become for us a Samuel. You are Eli to many children. May God bless you and the work you do in the lives of the children in your life and your care.

Ideas to Consider

- What is your church currently doing to encourage and support children in prayer?
- If encouraging children to develop their own relationship with God is more important than teaching children to pray, what changes need to take place in your children's ministry program/your home?
- What tools can you give children to help them speak to God?
- How are you encouraging children to listen to God?
- What are you doing to affirm children's encounters with God?

CHILDREN'S PRAYER GUIDE

Sally Langford

How do we teach our children to pray? Invite children to pray for others with the help of a pictorial prayer guide. Create this prayer guide during Sunday school or Vacation Bible School.

First, collect photographs of people who are important to the children. Children may bring photographs from home of family members, friends, and pets. Use a digital camera to take pictures at church of Sunday school teachers, pastors, and church staff. Assist the children as they clip additional pictures of interest from newspapers or magazines. Once the pictures are collected, the children may place them in a photo album and color or decorate the pages of the album with art.

After the children complete their pictorial prayer guides, show the children how to turn through the pages of the album, saying a prayer for each person pictured. Children may leave their pictorial prayer guides in the classroom in order to practice praying for others at class gatherings. In time, encourage children to take their prayer guides home, where each morning or night they may look at the photographs and say a prayer for each of their loved ones.

TEENS AND PRAYER

Leanne Ciampa Hadley

Leanne Ciampa Hadley, president and founder of the First Steps Spirituality Center and United Methodist pastor, says it is important to accept teens' styles of prayer even when they are not our styles. We can help teens to grow in their relationship with God by encouraging them to find authentic ways of expressing themselves through prayer.

The teen years are private years filled with change, confusion, and soul-searching. It makes sense that as teens turn inward, trying to figure out who they are, they often become more private and less forthcoming in sharing their prayers. But this does not mean that they do not pray. In fact, my experience with teens is that they pray and pray hard!

Helping teens to pray, especially during the difficult times of their lives, means helping them to understand the real goal of prayer—which is a relationship with God—and helping them to find authentic ways to pray.

Be an Encourager

Teens are in the process of finding their own voice and their own relationship with God. That means we must step out of their way and stop trying to control how they pray. Our role is to teach less and to become encouragers for them to pray. Reminding them that prayer takes many forms will help them to embrace prayer when life seems difficult or overwhelming. Writing a poem or song, painting a picture, or creating a bouquet of flowers can be forms of prayer. Reminding teens that prayer is not a thing but a relationship with God encourages them to express themselves to God in whatever ways feel natural for them.

Our role is to teach less and to become encouragers for [teens] to pray.

Listen Without Judgment

One of the greatest gifts we can give to teens is to listen without judgment when they do share their prayers with us. It is painful to hear them speak about broken relationships, feeling ugly and unattractive, and wondering what to do with their lives. We often feel the need to solve their problems, convince them that the pain will pass, and tell them that it won't matter ten years from now. We do all we can to make them feel better. Instead of fixing their pain, our best response should be to remind them that God understands their pain and is always there to listen and support them. As we model simply being present, listening, and accepting their pain as real and important to them, we model the loving presence of God.

Help to Make Prayer a Part of Everyday Life

Like all of us, during times of stress or pain or crisis, teens often have difficulty praying. They would rather keep their mind off their problems and pain by trying not to think about it and distracting themselves by hanging out with their friends or playing video games. However, it is in the stillness of prayer that they will find the healing presence of God. This is why it is so important that we help make prayer a part of the everyday lives of teens. If they experience and discover a solid relationship with God in the ordinary times, then in times of crisis and pain they will be comfortable with prayer and readily turn to God.

Instead of fixing their pain, our best response should be to remind them that God understands their pain and is always there to listen and support them.

Use Prayer Tools

Prayer tools are an effective way to help teens slow down, be still, and focus on God. Giving teens tangible items they can use to express their prayers assures them that we trust their ability to communicate and listen to God. It also helps them begin expressing themselves to God in their unique way. During the confusing teen years, it is sometimes difficult for teens to find words to express their stress or pain. Often drawing a symbol or writing the symbolic language of poetry and songs or laying a flower beside a grave say what words alone cannot. Giving teens a set of paints and a canvas or a new journal and pen gives them the freedom and medium to communicate their deepest feelings to God.

Here are some suggestions for prayer tools for teens:

- Give teens some beautiful beads and wire and invite them to make prayer beads they can use to count their blessings or repeat a line of Scripture over and over as a prayer. This prayer can be adapted in times of crisis so that each bead represents a support person who surrounds the teen as he or she heals. Or if a loved one is ill or has died, a teen might string one bead for each letter in the loved one's name. (To read more on prayer beads, see Sally Dyck's article on page 156.)
- Invite teens to read from Psalms, find a verse that speaks to his or her pain, and then paint or draw that verse. They can use paint, clay, or any art medium to spend time hearing, reflecting on, and experiencing God's words. In times of pain, repeating the same prayer can be extremely powerful!

- Give teens Bibles and highlighters and invite them to search for passages where God might be speaking to them. These verses invite them to be present with God and God's promises and to hear God speak to them. In times of pain, these verses might bring hope and healing.
- Have teens make a CD of songs that put into words what they would like to say to God or hear from God. Prayer CDs lead to wonderful prayer times as teens sit in the presence of God through the vehicle of music. In times of crisis, teens can make a CD of specific songs and music that bring healing and hope.
- Give teens a candle and invite them to light it to remind them of God's presence and light. This allows them to become comfortable with stillness and quiet, contemplative prayer. In times of pain, a candle can be used to remind teens that, even in the darkest night, God's light of hope and healing still shines.
- Many teens love jewelry and often wear pins, bracelets, or ribbons for a specific reason or cause. Give teens ribbon, beads, and string to make bracelets or pins as reminders to pray, or as reminders that God loves them and is always willing to hear their prayers. These same pins and bracelets can be made and worn in memory of a friend who has died. Each time they wear it, it can remind them that God is with them and will be with them as they heal.
- Have teens create boxes and fill them with words and images they have glued to small cardboard shapes. Teens can then form prayers by arranging the words and images in their own order, helping them to express themselves to God. Be sure to include words that capture pain as well as joy so that all the feelings teens experience in good or sad times can be expressed.

When we give teens creative, inviting, and expressive ways to be in the presence of God, we are increasing the likelihood that they will make time to pray and form a lasting and personal relationship with God. We are teaching them that they can turn to God at all times in their lives, including those that are the most painful. Let me share a couple of examples.

A young woman was diagnosed with cancer. Her teen daughters were naturally afraid. The adults around them did all they could to help them feel better. They brought them their favorite foods to eat, took them to the movies, and gave them gift cards, but the most healing gifts were new notebooks with black pages and sets of metallic gel pens. In those books the girls drew pictures and wrote poems and prayers. The notebooks were a safe place to pour out their feelings.

The son of a friend of mine loves to play the guitar and write songs. When his father died, his mother gave him his father's guitar. He played it, wrote songs, and expressed the very core of his pain.

Encourage "Safe" Prayer and Ritual in Times of Crisis

Sometimes teens in crisis find prayer difficult because they are ashamed of the feelings they are experiencing. If a teen feels guilt after the death of a loved one, he or she often holds it inside because it is painful to admit. Likewise, if a teen's parents are divorcing, the teen might feel intense anger and yet hold it in because he or she has been taught that being really angry and even hating, even for the time being, is wrong.

During times of crisis such as these, it is helpful to give teens a way to pray so that their prayers are "safe" and will not be found or read by others.

When we give teens creative, inviting, and expressive ways to be in the presence of God, we are increasing the likelihood that they will make time to pray and form a lasting and personal relationship with God.

Teens can write their prayers in a sandbox and them wipe them away. They can say what they need to say without anyone being able to discover it or read it. Flash paper or paper that dissolves in water are also great ways to help teens write down their prayers and then give them to God. In a flash they are burned or dissolved in water so that no one can ever read them. This gives teens the opportunity to put their prayers into words and assures them that what they say is between God and them, providing the privacy they need.

Ritual is another powerful way to help teens come together, pray, and find comfort. Rituals often naturally occur, such as placing flowers and mementos in the front yard of a friend who has died or sitting around a bonfire and sharing memories and prayers. These are meaningful and healing rituals for teens.

Not long ago, I was called to a hospital where a teenage boy lay in a bed after attempting suicide. I rode the elevator up to the ICU floor and got off. I knew where the teen's room was because I could hear the crying of the visiting teens who had gathered around his bed. They were crying and encouraging him to live. When I entered and told them I was his minister, almost in unison they asked me to say a prayer. They formed a circle around his bed, holding hands. I prayed and they sobbed.

Despite all the prayers and tears, this teen died. I went to his home to visit his family and, again, I found the house not because I knew where it was but because his yard was covered with bouquets of flowers and prayers hand-written on sheets of notebook paper, post-it notes, and cards. At the funeral, these teens spoke about his life, reading poems they had written and sharing a PowerPoint presentation they had made of his life.

When a teen in my community was killed in a tragic accident, her friends got together and had her signature tattooed on their wrists. They asked me to stop by the tattoo parlor where they were having it done. I did so, not because I think tattoos are a great idea, but because I knew how important it was to them that I come. I watched silently as, one at a time, they had the signature placed on their wrists; and it was one of the holiest things I have ever experienced. The marks on their wrists are more than tattoos; they are a reminder that their friend is in heaven and that they will all be together again someday. They are reminders that life is precious and that they need to love their lives to the fullest. These tattoos are their prayers. A tattoo may not be the way I would choose to pray, but for these teens it is a prayer nonetheless; and through these prayers they will heal!

Emphasize Prayer as Relationship

Prayer is not a thing; it is a relationship. Prayer is communicating with God and being in the presence of God to receive God's healing, love, and support. Whether or not teens pray often is strengthened by the attitudes of the adults around them. When we accept their styles of prayer, even when it is not our style, and when we encourage them to pray by giving them ways that they can authentically express themselves, we help them communicate with God and receive God's healing.

Whether or not teens pray often is strengthened by the attitudes of the adults around them.

Ideas to Consider

- How does your church help teens to find authentic ways of praying? In what ways are you equipping parents to do this?
- If our role related to prayer during the teen years is to teach less and encourage more, how well are you doing (as a church, youth minister, Sunday school teacher, parent, other)? What specific things are you doing or can you do to encourage teens to pray?
- What prayer tools have you used with teens? What new creative and expressive ways can you find to invite them to communicate with God?
- What are you doing to create a "safe" environment for prayer? What are some "safe" ways of praying you can use with teens?
- What rituals are part of your prayer ministry with teens?

PRAYER IDEAS FOR YOUTH

Sally Langford

Youth appreciate having age-appropriate opportunities for learning how to pray. At one local church, the pastor and youth Sunday school teacher designed a five-week lesson plan on prayer. Each week the youth began class by praying together the Lord's Prayer; they ended class by reciting the blessing found in Numbers 6:24-26. The youth also created their own prayer journals, which they continued to use long after the unit on prayer ended. In addition to discussing prayer basics, such as various postures for prayer, they delved into hard topics, such as stumbling blocks to prayer and unanswered prayer. During the five-week study, the youth interviewed and prayed with older church members they considered "prayer warriors." At the conclusion of the study, the youth invited the congregation to walk with them during Sunday morning worship through seven stations set up for multisensory prayer.

Youth appreciate having age-appropriate opportunities for learning how to pray.

Here's one idea for leading youth in multisensory prayer. Read aloud a brief passage of Scripture and invite class members to pray and meditate on the words. Provide Bibles so that everyone can read and reread the passage individually. Instruct each class member to choose one word of significance from the Scripture and then to draw a picture that uses that word as the focus of the art. Provide art supplies appropriate for the class, and allow time for class members to share their works of art with one another.

Group prayer is another way for youth to experience prayer. One youth group enjoys what it calls "crazy prayer." Divide the group into teams of two or three and ask the teams to share prayer concerns from the week with one another. Call for quiet. Each team begins when ready to pray aloud for its own prayer concerns. One or two teams usually will begin praying first, and before long all the teams are praying aloud simultaneously. Gradually, the teams conclude their prayers.

"GT" or "God's Time" is another idea for incorporating prayer into weekly youth gatherings. After the youth have had plenty of time to talk and laugh together, the leader calls out, "GT! It's God's Time!" The youth gather in a circle and are quiet and meditative. After a time of silence, the youth share concerns and celebrations with one another. The leader or a youth member then closes GT with a spoken prayer.

PRAYER FOR ALL PERSONALITY TYPES:
Supporting Spiritual Extroverts

Nancy C. Reeves

Nancy C. Reeves *is a ical psychologist, spiri-' director, poet, and au-r. She is director of the nd Loss Clinic, adjunct lty at the University of toria and Santa Clara niversity, and conducts any lectures and work-ps internationally. For re information, sugges-s, and stories related to porting spiritual extro-s in faith communities, er book* Spirituality for xtroverts (And Tips for Those Who Love Them) *(Abingdon Press, 2008).*

There are more extroverts than introverts in the world, yet many church prayer programs and services encourage solely introvert prayer practices—postures or positions of prayer that are more contemplative than active. Perhaps this is why spiritual communities often contain a higher percentage of introverts. In most congregations, young extroverts are welcomed and encouraged in the various child-centered programs, yet they feel out of place in worship. Daniel, who is 22 years old, told me about his experience:

My bouncy energy and love of meeting new people fit really well in Sunday school and youth group. I connect with God most often through other people or in nature. I like praying with groups, but I want to share my prayer experiences afterward. When I became an adult and sat in the regular service, I often felt bored and jittery. I wanted to talk with other people about my take on the Scriptures or the sermon I had heard. For a while, I just slept in on Sunday morning, but that didn't feel really good. That church was a home for me. I knew and cared for so many of those people. So, I went out into the woods and talked with God for a long time. An idea was put into my head and heart that has solved the problem for me. I now spend my Sunday mornings with the Kindergarten/Grade 1 class!

Daniel is not unique. In my research, which resulted in the book *Spirituality for Extroverts (And Tips for Those Who Love Them)*, many of the folks who completed my questionnaire reported feeling unwelcome, or simply tolerated, in their congregations. They also had the impression that introverts inherently have a deeper spirituality because they are more comfortable "turning inward."

Does the church have a place for extroverts? Of course it does, and yet knowledge is necessary for there to be a healthy intermingling of both orientations.

Understanding Basic Differences

A beginning point is understanding some of the basic differences between extroverts and introverts. As an extrovert myself, I have firsthand knowledge of extrovert tendencies. We extroverts are folks whose attention and energy are often directed to the outside world of people and things. We are more prone to action than contemplation. We make friends readily, adjust easily to social situations, and generally show warm interest in our surroundings.

In contrast, introverts are people whose attention and energy are more often focused on the inner world of their own thoughts and feelings. Some introverts also tend to minimize their contact with other people.

In most congregations, young extroverts . . . feel out of place in worship. Some recent brain research seems to indicate that extroversion is hardwired into us before birth. There also are indications that extroversion can be learned. A number of people in my study wrote of how they have become more or less extroverted over the years. It may be that if we consistently act in an outgoing manner, we can actually learn to be extroverted. In any case, as with so much about being human, the answer is not solely one or the other. Extroversion is likely hardwired to some extent, and our developing personality, life experiences, family, and society have some effect, as well.

Encouraging Prayer Practices for Extroverts

Once we understand the basic differences between extroverts and introverts, we begin to recognize the need and value of prayer practices that are more suited for the extrovert personality. We find numerous examples in the Bible, such as the extroverted Miriam who danced, sang, and played her tambourine to the Lord in a prayer practice of gratitude.

In my questionnaire, I asked extroverts to list spiritual practices that nurtured them. Prayer and meditation were at the top of the list, however the descriptions of these practices often had an extrovert "flavor." Many people do an extroverted version of contemplative prayer in which they respond with an outpouring of love and gratitude to any "God touch"—any sense of divine presence, guidance, or infused love. The key difference here is an active response to an inner experience.

Extroverts also often prefer to pray in groups that give space for talking about the experience afterward. Cultivating spiritual friendships is also important. Singing and various types of moving prayer practices are high on the preferred list, as well.

Specific Suggestions

Overtly welcome both extroverts and introverts into church-run spiritual activities. For example, an early-morning weekday walking prayer group could meet in the church parking lot and split into two groups: one for people who want to walk together in silence, the other for those who find it enhances their prayer experience to share it verbally with others. Both orientations may think, "Look at the colors in that tree. Thank you God, for giving us such a beautiful world." Extroverts usually find it helpful to speak the words out loud. The two groups could rejoin for breakfast and socializing.

Extroverts often prefer to pray in groups that give space for talking about the experience afterward.

In Adult Sunday school or other sessions, give "processing" options, such as, "Let's spend ten minutes exploring this topic / Scripture / idea. You may wish to do this alone or find a partner or join a small group."

Sermon Idea

Many Scripture passages show an extroverted Jesus spending time with large groups of people. Other passages show a Jesus who needs quiet time. Talking about how Jesus was able to shift from introverted to extroverted energy will be affirming for extroverted listeners.

Addressing Some of the Challenges

There are a number of challenges extroverts face that can interfere with the benefit of any prayer practice. If these are not addressed and worked through, even the most extroverted prayer practice will have difficulty promoting a deeper connection with God.

In my research, I found that four of these challenges can make it difficult for the worship community to welcome the extrovert, and for the extrovert to be comfortable in the congregation. In an attempt to deal with these challenging tendencies, communities often try to encourage the extrovert to become more introverted. This may result in the extrovert feeling judged and leaving the congregation, or trying to fit in by pretending to be other than his or her true self. The solution that helps extroverts to mature spiritually and psychologically is to transform the unhealthy aspects of each tendency by providing prayer and worship experiences that move along the continuum of that tendency. In this way congregations can be instrumental in helping extroverts to reach a healthy place.

Challenge #1: Impulsivity
Solution: Encourage Spontaneity

We extroverts are always processing data. We also have a strong urge to share, contribute, and act. So when we find ourselves with a chance to speak, we may quickly say what's on our mind at that moment. This is impulsivity. The sharing may not be what we would say if we took even a few moments to consider our contribution. We may also act without thinking through the implications of our behaviors. Impulsivity keeps us in shallow waters of thought and action.

Spontaneity, the other end of this continuum, is indeed gracefully natural and unrestrained. People who are spontaneous are able to embrace the moment flexibly. They can sense and respond to that moment to meet their own or another's unexpected needs. People who act spontaneously see the reality of a situation and deal with it swiftly and decisively while being grounded in "divine flow." Spontaneous people know that some things need to be planned, and the planning enhances their spontaneity.

Specific Suggestions

When it is time for discussion during youth group meetings, workshops, or council meetings, invite everyone to be silent for a few moments before speaking. Explain that often extroverts say the first thought that comes to them, later wishing they had shared something else instead. Introverts may not really listen to the extrovert's initial contribution because they are still deciding what to say. So, taking a few moments of silence as a group helps introverts to get up to speed and help extroverts to go a little deeper before sharing.

Sermon Idea

A wonderful example of shifting from impulsivity to spontaneity is Simon Peter. He exhibits many examples of impulsivity in the Gospels. Then, in the Book of Acts, after some huge growth experiences, Peter demonstrates spontaneity. He still thinks and acts quickly, but he has developed an ability to quickly monitor and evaluate a situation. The spontaneous Peter is a powerful dynamic force for helping the young Christian church to become more inclusive and sensitive to the needs of others.

Challenge #2: Unfocused Chatter
Solution: Encourage Focused Talk

Do you know folks who tend to jump from topic to topic, bringing in a great amount of detail? Or do you know someone who frequently talks about the past in order to explain what is occurring in the present? Since extroverts benefit from processing out loud and place such a high value on relationships, we tend to make connections in our minds that result in lengthy recitations.

At the healthy end of this continuum, "focused talk" extroverts are clear about their goals in conversing and bring in enough detail or stories to illustrate their points in an interesting way. One workshop participant said, "I love it when my extrovert minister shares at meetings. She uses touching stories that make her points come alive. Her sharing helps me remember my own experiences."

Specific Suggestions

Being a role model for focused talk can be very useful in one-on-one contacts as well as in groups. Statements such as, "I'm going to explain my point by giving two examples," or "I just realized I've been talking for a few minutes. I'll be quiet now and give someone else a chance to talk," can show extroverts how to share appropriately.

Groups can include norms around giving everyone a chance to talk. When serving as a facilitator, I usually add, "I'm an extrovert, and I know that we extroverts can get excited and not realize how many stories we've told or how long we have been talking." Then I ask the group's permission to let me keep track of time and stop someone in order to give others a chance to speak.

Extroverts tend to find it helpful to process ideas out loud with others. Introverts tend to do that processing alone. A classic scenario is that a group comes together to make a decision, such as where to go for the annual church picnic. Suggestions have been sent around by email, and the introverts have come prepared to give their recommendations. The extroverts, however, want to discuss all the suggestions, and both groups become frustrated with each other. It can be helpful to set time for a brainstorming pre-meeting just before the regular meeting, which will attract and satisfy the extroverts. They will then be prepared with their recommendations when the introverts show up.

Extroverts tend to find it helpful to process ideas out loud with others.

Sermon Idea

No one wants to listen to a sermon that is "all over the place." Always be intentional and organized when planning and writing sermons. Write an outline and stick to it. Communicate to your listeners the purpose or main message of your sermon, clearly identifying each supporting point as you come to it. Use stories and anecdotes to illustrate your points and hold the interest of your listeners. These simple strategies will help your listeners not only to remember what they hear but also to apply it in their daily lives.

Challenge #3: Stimulation Junkie
Solution: Encourage Living a Multifaceted Spirituality

Brain research shows that extroverts need more stimulation than do introverts. Unhealthy extroverts tend to jump from one spiritual practice or congregation to another as soon as the "honeymoon" period is over. This can definitely result in a superficial spiritual life.

The healthy end of this continuum is living a multifaceted spirituality. Many of us extroverts feel a benefit in having a number of different spiritual practices in our lives at any one time. Just because a spiritual practice is enjoyable or beneficial, though, is not enough reason to include it as a frequent practice; more is not necessarily better. We need to evaluate how adding the practice will affect our other practices, our time, energy level, and other factors. We need to find a creative balance in our spiritual life.

Specific Suggestions

Organize a presentation for Sunday school or some other setting on how to choose a prayer practice. The key point of this presentation is that God invites us to the prayer practice that is best for us now. Over time, we may find that we stay with some practices briefly and with others for years. The presentation might cover spiritual discernment, how to "tune in" to God's guidance, and list a number of different practices, describing how each can be done with an introverted or extroverted "flavor."

A multisession course would expand the previous suggestion and provide opportunities for participants to practice a number of extroverted and introverted types of prayer.

Sermon Idea

"We have gifts that differ according to the grace given to us" (Romans 12:6). One of the gifts we have been given is our basic character. There is some evidence that we are born with an extroverted or introverted tendency. How can we honor and use this gift we have been given without thinking that the other tendency is better? This question speaks to the issue that introverts are often perceived to be more spiritual while extroverts are perceived to be better at service.

Challenge #4: Lost in Space
Solution: Encourage Befriending Silence

Do you know extroverts who won't let more than a second or two of silence go by without breaking it? Because extroverts are more comfortable with their energy directed outward, being silent can be a huge challenge, unlike introverts who view silence as their "happy place." If extroverts are unable to enjoy some silence, they are more likely to dominate conversations and not give introverts a chance to complete their need for internal processing. In my research, I found that many of my participants said that they became more comfortable with silence when introverts shared what the experience of silence was like for them. Without understanding how silence can be a good experience, extroverts view it as a "dead space" or punishment.

Extrovert energy is made to flow outward. To experience "good" silence, extroverts need to access the inward flowing introvert energy. The worship service actually is great

Because extroverts are more comfortable with their energy directed outward, being silent can be a huge challenge.

training ground for this, as there are times when introvert energy will help us live into the experience more fully, and times when extrovert energy will do so. If we are solely directed inward or outward during worship, we are missing the "full meal deal."

Specific Suggestions

Bulletins usually simply announce silent times, "There will be a few minutes of silence prior to the beginning of the service." Extroverts often have no idea what to do in the silence, so they end up reading the rest of the bulletin until "something happens." Adding the following can be helpful: "During this time you may wish to pray silently, or to become aware of the joys and concerns you wish to bring to God, or to turn your focus to a place of inner stillness where you can rest in God."

Sermon Idea

There are many Scripture passages that indicate the importance of quiet "alone time" with God, such as, "He said to them, 'Come away to a deserted place all by yourselves and rest a while'" (Mark 6:31). This is a good opportunity to talk about the importance of silence in our lives and to clarify that extroverts need to use introvert energy in order to enjoy and benefit from silence.

Becoming an Omnivert Like Jesus

I found in my research that some folks are able to be energized by the inner world as well as the outer. They can move to the orientation that is most useful for them at any given time. I call these folk omniverts. The prefix *omni* means "combining all." Each omnivert will have either an extroverted or introverted inclination.

I believe that abundant life is much more possible when we can become energized by both the inner and outer worlds. Let's look at an example of a healthy omnivert.

Jesus Christ began his public ministry during a party, a wedding feast at Cana. This is a scene that extroverts can relate to. In his ministry, Jesus surrounded himself with followers and went out of his way to meet new people. When some complained of his inclusive and frequent socializing, Jesus told his followers that it was impossible to please people who held onto rigid expectations of how one sent from God was to behave. He compared himself to his cousin, John the Baptist: "For John came neither eating nor drinking, and they say, 'He has a demon'; the Son of Man came eating and drinking, and they say, 'Look, a glutton and a drunkard, a friend of tax collectors and sinners!' Yet wisdom is vindicated by her deeds" (Matthew 11:18-19).

A healthy congregation welcomes and has room for a wide variety of prayer forms and experiences.

Jesus taught a relational theology: God is a loving parent who wants intimacy with all people. The prayer Jesus taught his followers to say begins with an assertion of the divine/human relationship. This, too, sounds like an extrovert. And yet Jesus also drew nurturance from an introverted place. He needed time alone. Even though many of his followers would have been honored to give Jesus a bed for the night, when he was in the Jerusalem area he preferred to teach in the temple during the day and spend the night on the Mount of Olives (Luke 21:37). Likewise, he encouraged his followers to take quiet rest time (Mark 6:30-32).

Any prayer practice can be done in an extroverted or introverted way. I believe a healthy congregation welcomes and has room for a wide variety of prayer forms and experiences. This gives introverts and extroverts opportunities to pray in ways that honor their preferred orientation as well as encourages them to move past their comfort zone in order to experience the richness of the other orientation. As omniverts, we have so many more prayer options open to us.

Ideas to Consider

- Are the prayer practices in your worship services and prayer programs more suited for introverts than extroverts (are they more contemplative than active)?
- How can you make your worship experience more welcoming to extroverts?

- What extroverted prayer practices might be incorporated into Sunday school, prayer programs, or other activities and events of the church?
- Of the four challenges that extroverts face, which does your church address most effectively, and how? Which does your church address least effectively, and why?
- If a healthy congregation welcomes and has room for a wide variety of prayer forms and experiences, how "healthy" would you say your church is on a scale of 1-10 (with 1 being very unhealthy and 10 being very healthy)?

PRAYER BEADS AS TEACHING TOOLS

Sally Dyck

Sally Dyck *is a bishop of The United Methodist Church serving in Minnesota. Here, she presents prayer beads as a tool for jump-starting, reviving, strengthening, or deepening one's prayer life.*

A number of years ago, I served as a director on the United Methodist General Board of Global Ministries. At one meeting, a woman from Norway named Tove showed me her prayer beads. She said that she used them in prayer on a regular basis. Six months later when I saw Tove again, I asked her if she would explain the prayer beads to me. She said that the beads are called *Fralsarkransen*, which means "the wreath of Christ" in Swedish. Then she described each bead to me and told me what to pray while holding it. That was over a decade ago, and my prayer life has never been the same since.

Every religious tradition except Protestantism uses some form of prayer beads. Each bead represents a different prayer point or concern. Holding each bead as you pray, beginning with the gold or God bead, helps to focus and structure your prayers. This practice is helpful because, as most of us experience in prayer, we tend to get lost in our own thoughts. When there is no organized structure to our prayers, we drift from one thing to another. Prayer beads help us to focus our thoughts; return to them when our minds and hearts wander; and have a structure that gives us a wider, fuller spectrum of prayer.

Prayer beads help us to focus our thoughts; return to them when our minds and hearts wander; and have a structure that gives us a wider, fuller spectrum of prayer.

It has been many years since I started using prayer beads. Although I do not always use prayer beads when I pray, I know where my beads are whenever I need or want them. From time to time, my prayer beads provide the focus and structure I need to revitalize or deepen my prayer life.

Many Uses, One Purpose

Over the years I have given prayer beads to many people. One staff member found the prayer beads to be so helpful in structuring his prayer time that he preached a sermon on it, and suddenly fifty people in the church wanted prayer beads!

My young adult niece has used prayer beads during transitional or difficult times in her life. She says that during a three-month trip to Australia and New Zealand, the beads were a force that guided her growth and reflection. Another family member told me that she uses her prayer beads mostly when she is walking in the mornings or evenings and when she's driving long distances alone. Sometimes she holds them when she's having difficulty falling asleep or getting back to sleep. The beads help her focus her prayers during these times of reflection or anxiety. She uses her beads to pray for herself and her loved ones, but she also assigns a purple bead to people she might otherwise forget about, such as those who are in the military. She says, "When I focus on the world bead, I pray especially for children all over the world to feel God's presence with them. This helps me realize how abundantly I am blessed and challenges me to look more closely at how I live and what I do or think that might make a difference, at least for some of them."

A friend of mine gave prayer beads to her four-year-old daughter. Though my friend modified the beads slightly, the practice provided the same kind of structure for her young daughter's prayers. Now her daughter is a pre-adolescent. Although she doesn't always use the beads, she says just holding them gives her comfort.

One year I gave my staff prayer beads for Christmas. Some used them and even expressed that the beads were meaningful. Others didn't say anything about them. A couple of years later, I went into one staff person's office and saw the beads on her desk. When I asked about them, she indicated that she wanted to figure out a way to give a set to her mother. I noted that she wasn't letting go of her own set, so I gave her another set! She said, "We are constantly bombarded with images, data, information, and messages. The beads help me tune out the distractions of life. The ability to hold and touch something helps me to be quiet and listen to God's voice as I seek to understand and respond. Sometimes when I can't find words, just touching each bead seems like praying—but without words."

Praying is often difficult in times of adversity and suffering. We tend to be so upset that we don't have words. Then we begin to feel **Prayer beads give us a way to pray when there are no words.** that we simply are unable to pray. I agree with my staff member that simply having an awareness of what each bead means, instead of having to say words, has given me great comfort over the years. Prayer beads give us a way to pray when there are no words.

The same staff member reflected, "The beads help me to be more disciplined because they are so flexible. I can use them anywhere and anytime. I can pray the beads on the bus ride to or from work. I can use them at home, in the office, or someone else's office when I'm early for a meeting. I can take five minutes per bead or five minutes in total. I like to use repeated phrases, such as a litany, between each main bead. I can pray them in any order. The reminder of what each bead is for is in a memo document in my smart phone so I can refer to it anytime and anywhere."

While this staff person is a strong introvert, another staff person who is an extrovert commented that the beads helped to focus his attention. Regardless of personality temperament or manner of use, prayer beads have one unifying purpose: to provide focus and structure for prayer.

Making Prayer Beads

Prayer beads can be fancy or simple. When making prayer beads with groups, I often buy the cheapest beads I can find at the store and then instruct participants to go to a nice craft or bead store to find just the right beads for them. Usually I begin by explaining to men that prayer beads are not bracelets! The beads should just slip over the fingers so that they circle the outer hand and palm; they are not to be worn as a bracelet on one's wrist. They are not jewelry but an aid to prayer.

Over the years since my friend Tove shared the description of her prayer beads with me, I have revised the plan or pattern many times and "made it my own." The following guide is my revision. I encourage you to begin with this guide and make your own modifications as needed, just as I did with Tove's original description.

A Pattern for Prayer Beads

Big Gold Bead: God
Offer prayers of thanksgiving and praise to God.

Clear Bead: Self
Say prayers for yourself.

Triangular Bead: Worries
Tell all your worries to God and leave them there.

Light Blue Bead: Silence
Be silent and listen for God.

Wooden Bead: Desert of Faith
What are you working on in your faith?

Clear with Black Bead: Night and Day
What are you struggling with in your life? Offer it to God.

Green Bead: Your Special Concern
Pray about the most pressing or important concern to you personally.

2 Red Beads: People to Love
Pray for those you love and those you have trouble loving.

3 Purple Beads: Additional Concerns
Lift up three additional concerns.

Deep Blue or Turquoise Bead: The World
Pray for world concerns.

(Note: Above image is also available in color on the DVD-Rom.)

Ideas to Consider

- How can prayer beads help us to focus, structure, and enhance our prayer life?
- What are some different times and ways to use prayer beads?
- What might be some times and opportunities in your church for introducing and making prayer beads?

15 WAYS TO PRAY IN A SMALL GROUP

Laurie Barnes

[See the full article on the DVD-Rom.]

Some people feel out of their "comfort zone" when asked to pray out loud. But as Jesus taught us in the parable of the pharisee and tax collector (Luke 18:9-14), prayers do not need to be long or verbose to be effective. Ideally, not just the leader but all members of the group should be included in the opportunity to pray to God on behalf of and for the group. Following are fifteen ways that your small group can involve all of its members in prayer:

1. **Prayer partners.** Encourage partners to communicate with each other once a week outside of the group meeting with a card, email, or phone call.
2. **Joys and concerns.** Stand in a circle – one person prays.
3. **Joys and concerns – variation.** Stand in a circle – all who feel led to pray are encouraged to pray (also called "popcorn prayer").
4. **Create a prayer focus – example "Thankful" prayers.** Holding hands, everyone is asked to express one thing for which they are thankful.
5. **One-sentence intercessory prayers.** In a circle, everyone is asked to pray out loud a one-sentence prayer giving thanks for the person on their left.
6. **Lay hands on someone and pray.**
7. **Praying by proxy.** For members unable to be in class, put an empty chair in the circle, pray for them as if they were present and sitting in the chair.
8. **Assigned (in advance) opening prayer.** Preparing a prayer in advance is an encouragement to many who do not feel comfortable praying out loud.
9. **Prayer journal.** Record the joys and concerns in a prayer journal each meeting. Share and reflect on all the answered prayers at the end of the year.
10. **Email prayer concerns.** Have one or two volunteers commit to sending out the joys and concerns to group members by email each week.
11. **Include a prayer in the worship bulletin each week.**
12. **Use the Psalms.** Assign small-group members a psalm to use as a prayer to open or close the small-group meeting.
13. **Directed prayer in the A.C.T.S. format** (**a**doration, **c**onfession, **t**hanksgiving, **s**upplication)
14. **Use a prayer book.** Members take turns selecting prayers/devotions from a book of written prayers to open the group meeting time each week.
15. **Time of silent corporate prayer.** After joys and concerns are shared, each member prays for specific requests during a time of silent prayer.

These are just some of the many ways that small-group leaders can help their group members grow in their knowledge and familiarity with the powerful experience of prayer. My hope and prayer is that by helping group members become more comfortable with prayer, each and every participant in a small group will begin to add or increase prayer as a part of his or her daily life.

V.

BECOMING A PRAYING CONGREGATION AT HOME

A praying congregation requires praying households. Only when families are living a life of prayer outside the church walls does prayer truly become a vital part of what happens within the church. With the competing demands and busy schedules families face on a daily basis, parents and other caregivers need help and encouragement for teaching and modeling prayer in the home more than ever before. Equipping families to become praying households is one of the most crucial tasks facing the church today. As you seek to find ways your congregation may address this challenge, consider the following:

- How might the life of your congregation be impacted if more families were to begin praying together at home?
- How does your congregation encourage and facilitate prayer in the home?
- Practically speaking, how do you equip parents and other caregivers to teach and model prayer at home? Are you providing new and creative prayer tips and tools, or are you using the same old approach?
- What are you doing to encourage couples to pray together on a regular basis?

Articles:

ENCOURAGING PRAYING HOUSEHOLDS

Betty Shannon Cloyd

ty Shannon Cloyd is aconal minister in The ed Methodist Church, a nsultant in prayer and ual formation, and the author of Parents and ndparents as Spiritual les *(Upper Room, 2000) d* Children and Prayer *er Room, 1997). In this icle she explores how to lop and maintain a life prayer within the home ite busy schedules and competing priorities.*

In the book of Acts, the Apostle Paul encouraged the Athenians to believe that "God is not far from each one of us" (Acts 17:27b). He continued his persuasive argument about the nearness of God by saying, "In him we live and move and have our being" (Acts 17:28a). If we today are to have praying households, this is the first concept that we must fully understand: God is near each one of us, and all of us live out our days in God's great encompassing and unfailing love. Our response to God's initial love for us is the beginning point of prayer. By communicating with God through prayer, we stay in touch with the great reality that God is, truly, the ground of our being.

Developing a Life of Prayer

In our busy, noisy lives, the question is, of course, how do we manage to do this? How do we, as parents, grandparents, and other caregivers, find the silence, solitude, and time we need in order to be a praying person ourselves? To be a praying person oneself is the first step in encouraging a praying household, because children learn best by our modeling; and it is very difficult, if not impossible, to share what we do not have.

There are many ways to get started in a life of prayer. One way is to set aside some quiet time every day when you can be alone with God. This might be only fifteen minutes, or longer if you can manage. It is helpful if you can find time for prayer in the morning, but if not, anytime during the day or evening will suffice. During this time, seek to remember that you are in God's presence and that God cares about your daily life and the specific needs of you and your family.

An extremely helpful tool for entering into prayer is to find some verse of Scripture that catches your interest and speaks to you. Read it slowly, savoring the words and letting them sink into your heart and

To be a praying person oneself is the first step in encouraging a praying household, because children learn best by our modeling; and it is very difficult, if not impossible, to share what we do not have.

soul. Tell God your needs and the needs of each person in the home, calling each by name. Remember that prayer is both talking to God and listening to God; so, end your time of devotion in silence, listening for what God has to say to you. Then thank God for the time you have spent together. Take something from your prayer time with you into the day or evening; this can be a word from the Scripture or an insight from your time in prayer.

Of course, there are many other ways to nurture your own prayer life. As your prayer life becomes stronger, you will be equipped to strengthen the prayer life of your household. Some of the ways you can do that include the following:

- Pray short verses of Scripture throughout the day, remembering that we can pray anywhere and anytime about anything.
- Keep a journal to enhance your prayer life. In it, record your thoughts and feelings about your encounters with God or note insights from your prayer time.
- Maintain a prayer card, listing those for whom you are praying and their specific needs. Also note when and how these prayers are answered.
- Read and pray the great prayers of those who have gone before us. These can be found easily in a variety of prayer books and hymn books.
- Go into each family member's room every day and pray for his or her particular needs. I have found it helpful to kneel at the bedside of each person, because being on our knees before God for those we love is a rewarding and humbling experience. Praying in secret for those we love has a powerful effect on them and on us.
- Write short "pocket prayers" and tuck them into appropriate family members' pockets, backpacks, briefcases, lunch sacks, and so forth.
- Use breath prayers composed of short sentences, slowly breathing the words in and out. Some examples are "Lord, have mercy," "Holy Spirit, fill me," and "Be near me, Lord Jesus."

Theophan the Recluse has said, "To pray is to descend with the mind into the heart, and there to stand before the face of the Lord, ever-present, all seeing, within you."[32] As we commit our lives to prayer, we grow in the knowledge that God is ever-present and that in God we live and move and have our being.

Making Prayer Part of Everyday Life

We turn now to the question of how to encourage and maintain a praying household. Again, we are faced with vastly competing priorities, especially when we consider the busy schedules of each family member: jobs, sports activities, school and homework, after-school events, play dates, and so forth. Our days are filled, but not always fulfilled. We long for that "something" that gives life meaning and purpose. The great saints of the past witness to the truth that what we are missing in our lives is a relationship with God, and prayer is the key to that relationship. Prayer is not about formulas or methods or forms. It is about a

Our days are filled, but not always fulfilled. . . . The great saints of the past witness to the truth that what we are missing in our lives is a relationship with God, and prayer is the key to that relationship.

personal, ongoing relationship with the One who created us and longs to be in communication with us.

Pray Often

It is important that we make prayer a natural part of the everyday life of the family, such as before meals, at bedtime, and at any other time that seems appropriate. When thinking of a definition of prayer for children, I like to use this one: Prayer is using our own words to talk with God and to listen to God at any time, at any place, and about anything.[33] It is important to stress to children (and adults) that they do not need to use lofty phrases; God understands their own words and is always ready to listen to anything they want to bring to God in prayer.

Give Parting Blessings

Some families like to bless one another as they are leaving the house for their various daily activities. It is a loving gesture to put one's hand on a loved one's head and say simply, "The Lord bless you and keep you." I believe it gives family members great comfort to know that God is keeping them in God's care.

Have Family Devotions

As a household, be intentional about having devotions or "faith breaks" together as many times a week as possible. It might be unrealistic to think that you can manage this every day, but at least strive for as many days as possible. Set aside a few minutes when all can gather. Turn off the TV and all electronic games and devices, and let the answering machine pick up all calls. Silence is so important, because it becomes the soil in which our prayer life may flourish and grow.

Choose someone to read a portion of Scripture and discuss briefly its meaning for the family. Sing a hymn or chorus that is familiar to all. Singing hymns of praise can be a wonderful family tradition, even if there are no trained voices in the group! The words and tunes of hymns of praise remain with us to well up joyfully at other times in our lives. I remember when I was babysitting our oldest grandson, who was three at the time, and we were taking a short trip. He was in the back buckled in his car seat as we rolled along. Suddenly he burst forth singing in his childlike voice, "Praise God from whom all blessings flow!" It was a touching moment for my husband and me.

During the devotion or "faith break," it is important to have a family prayer card. It might include names of friends of the family who have special needs, ministers of your church, those who are homebound or ill in your church, and members of the household and their needs. If a member of the family feels shy about praying aloud, it is best not to put the person on the spot by calling on him or her to pray. At first, if there is no one who is comfortable praying aloud, have someone read the names on the prayer card and follow each with a period of silent prayer. Close with praying in unison a short prayer that has been decided upon beforehand. As time goes on, gradually members of the household will become more comfortable praying aloud.

Plan Acts of Mercy

Another way we can encourage prayer life in our home is by doing acts of mercy together. Often God calls upon us to "put feet on our prayers," because God uses us to help do God's work in the world. If your family has been praying for someone who is sick or homebound or has some other need, gather as a group to prepare and deliver a fruit basket or meal or box of helpful household items or clothes. Be intentional about instilling values of caring and sharing in your home, because somehow these values insulate children from some of the toxins of life.

Make Rituals and Celebrations Part of Daily Life

It is extremely important to incorporate rituals and celebrations into the daily life of the family. These events help relieve the monotony and "everydayness" of life and give grounding and a sense of security to family members' lives. Rituals and celebrations also are a way to incorporate more opportunities for prayer into the home. They give us the opportunity to say unequivocally, "This is what we do in our family. This is what we believe."

All rituals and celebrations should be entered into with the acknowledgement of God's loving presence and overarching providential care. Some of these rituals might include having birthday celebrations, lighting the four candles during Advent, using a Christ candle during Lent and Easter, lighting a candle on All Saint's Day for some loved one who has died, having special baptismal celebrations, and celebrating New Year's Day by remembering blessings of the past year.

Families also can create their own rituals to commemorate special events in the family's life. These events might include occasions when a difficult school project is completed, when someone receives a significant award or honor, when a pet dies, when a child reaches some desired goal, or when the school year is beginning or ending. Candles, balloons, banners, and cards will enhance any event. The ritual should always include a prayer of thanks for God's grace and blessings.

In her book *The Shelter of Each Other*, Mary Pipher says that when we get too busy, rituals are the first thing to go.[34] In our busy lives we must remember to keep and cherish the rituals and celebrations that add so much to life and make us who we are.

Practice Hospitality

Another way we can encourage a praying household is by practicing the Benedictine commitment to hospitality. Learn to welcome God by welcoming others. It is such a broadening experience to let the home be a refuge and outreach, not only for biological kin but also for the wider community. It is especially meaningful when we open our homes to those who have no one else to love them. My own children have learned so much about God's wider world as we welcomed persons of other races, cultures, and languages. By practicing hospitality, their concept of God grew and expanded, as did their concept of prayer. It grew from praying for "me and mine" to praying for the whole world.

Incorporate rituals and celebrations into the daily life of the family. These events help relieve the monotony and "everydayness" of life and give grounding and a sense of security to family members' lives.

Spend One-on-One Time With Each Child

Another way to nurture the prayer life of children is to spend some special time with each child every week. Set aside a certain time and let the child come to think of it as his or her time with you. You certainly do not have to pray all the time you are together, but a short prayer for the child and his or her needs would be a part of this time. Whatever you do during that time together, the main focus should be listening to the child and reading "between the lines" for anything he or she wants to share with you. If possible, use the same time each week so the child comes to know that Tuesdays at 3:00, for example, is his or her time with Mom or Dad (or Grandma, Grandpa, Aunt Mary, Uncle Joe, etc.). Susannah Wesley had nineteen children, ten of whom lived to adulthood, and she managed to have a special time each week with each child. Our society has changed drastically since her time, but with persistent effort, this is a practice worth considering.

Jean-Pierre de Caussade tells us that we must learn to live in the sacrament of the present moment.

Be Present to the Present Moment

A word needs to be mentioned about the need for being present to the present moment in our lives. The days and years go by so quickly, and we must overcome the apathy that lulls us into a "when-then" mentality. That is, don't be tempted to say, "*When* the baby is older, *then* we can have a time of family prayer," or "*When* soccer season is over, *then* we will have time to help persons in need." Jean-Pierre de Caussade tells us that we must learn to live in the sacrament of the present moment.[35] To me, seeing the preciousness and sacramental nature of each present moment is a wonderful way of approaching life, and these moments are repeated over and over again during our lifetime.

Worship Together Regularly

In order to be a praying household, it is extremely important that the family worship together on a regular basis. Talk often about the elements of worship—the symbols employed, the liturgy involved, the seasonal liturgical colors used. Speak of the Scripture read, the sermon preached, and the prayers of the people, especially remembering those mentioned who are sick and in need. Remember to add them to your family prayer card so that you can pray for them during the week.

Look to the Church for Resources

The church also is a great resource for enhancing the prayer life of the home. Watch for announcements of classes or workshops on prayer, either in your church or in the community. If your church has a library, look for books on prayer and the spiritual life. Read church newsletters carefully as they often contain helpful articles relating to prayer. If you have questions about prayer, make an appointment with one of your pastors or other staff members for help with your needs.

Make a Commitment to Pray With and for Your Family

One way to be intentional about praying for our families is to make a written covenant or promise between oneself and God. Each individual in the family could write and sign his or her own covenant or promise, but it is especially important for the parents or guardian in charge to do so. The written promise does not have to be anything elaborate; one or two components would be sufficient. An example might be:

1) I will pray daily for each member of my household, and 2) I will strive with God's help to teach my children to pray and to have an ongoing relationship with God.

When we sign a holy commitment before God, it strengthens our resolve to keep that promise. (If you would like more information about writing and signing a written promise with God, see "The Hannah Promise" and "The Lois Promise" in *Parents and Grandparents as Spiritual Guides: Nurturing Children of the Promise* [Upper Room, 2000].) Review your covenant or promise frequently to see if you are keeping it faithfully, and feel free to revise it as needed.

The Difference Prayer Makes

In closing, I feel I must add a disclaimer. Am I saying that if we strive diligently to have a praying household that the dove of peace will rest over our homes? Am I saying that our children suddenly will become little saints or that there will be no serious illness among our loved ones, no disappointments, no job losses, no financial difficulties, no frustrations, no valleys? The answer is a resounding "No!" Just because we pray and try to follow God's will does not mean that we are assured of any of these things.

Prayer empowers us and gives us the courage to know that we can face life courageously because God is with us in it.

What difference does prayer really make, then? What prayer does is give us the assurance that God will be with us in the good and in the bad, in sad times and in happy times, in sickness and in health, in living and in dying. Prayer and our ongoing relationship with God give us a solid foundation to help us face whatever life brings. Prayer empowers us and gives us the courage to know that we can face life courageously because God is with us in it; for truly, it is in God and with God that we live and move and have our being.

Ideas to Consider

- Parents, grandparents, and other caregivers cannot cultivate praying households unless they are praying persons themselves. How does your church encourage and assist adults in cultivating their own life of prayer?
- What is the focus of prayer instruction and practice in your congregation? Is it more about formulas, methods, and forms than it is about a personal, ongoing relationship with God? How can you ensure that the latter focus or purpose is clearly communicated?
- What practical instruction or help does your church provide for making prayer a part of everyday family life? What models and resources might you provide?
- Is worship in your congregation "family friendly"? Are there changes that might help to encourage and equip families as they worship together?
- How important is prayer in the home to the health of your congregation? What can you do to be more encouraging and supportive to families in this area?
- Prayer is not an insurance policy against bad times; it gives us the solid foundation to help us face them.

PRAYING AT HOME

Leanne Ciampa Hadley

Leanne Ciampa Hadley, *president and founder of the First Steps Spirituality Center and United Methodist pastor, says that prayer at home is as important as prayer at church. In this article, she presents some practical ways to make prayer a part of everyday family life.*

The Bible tells us very little about the childhood of Jesus. The Scriptures tell us about his birth, that he was blessed as a baby, that he spent time in Egypt with his parents, that he grew up the child of a carpenter, and that he got lost in Jerusalem as a child. We also know something about Jesus' childhood because we know how Jewish households operated at that time. We know that on each Friday night, his mother lit holy candles and sabbath was celebrated with prayers and songs, not at the synagogue, but in his home. We know that a *mezuzah*, a tiny box containing the words of the Shema (Deuteronomy 6:4), hung on the doorpost of his home, and that he would touch it to remind him that he was a child of God each time he left and returned home. Because we know these things about Jesus' childhood, we know that he prayed at home as a child much more than he did at the temple or synagogue.

Using the childhood home of Jesus as an example, we need to make prayer at home as centrally important as prayer at church. In fact, praying once a week at church is simply not enough time to make prayer a part of children's lives.

1. Decide That Praying at Home Is Important

The first step in praying at home is deciding that it is important. We are busy! We come home tired from work and there are soccer games to go to, homework to check, and emails to return. For many of us, trying to add one more thing to our lives seems impossible. We must remember, however, that praying together as a family is important, and that learning lifelong skills requires repetition. Children learn math every day so that they

When we pray at home with our children . . . it lays a foundation for prayer to be a central part of their adult lives.

will remember how to do math when needed—not just now, but throughout their lives. It is the same with prayer. When we pray at home with our children, it not only helps them right now; it lays a foundation for prayer to be a central part of their adult lives.

2. Create Times and Places for Praying as a Family

Once we have decided that praying at home is important, we need to understand that it will not happen if we do not have set times to pray together as families. I encourage you to create spaces and times for prayer based on your family's lifestyle. Look for those times in the rhythm of your family's schedule where prayer time more naturally fits. Perhaps you play games on Friday nights. That would be a great time to work in prayer time. Perhaps you eat dinner together each Sunday night. That would be a natural time to add in family prayer time. Perhaps you tuck your kids into bed each night and read stories. That is a natural time and place to have prayer.

There are many ways you can pray together. One way is to take turns having each person say the prayer. Another is to read Scripture aloud and then sit quietly in contemplative prayer. After a few moments, have anyone who wants to share, share. Another form of prayer is to place a blessing cup on your dinner table and pass it to each person. Each person names a blessing that happened during the day or week as a prayer of gratitude to God. Lighting sacred candles each night to acknowledge God's presence is another form of prayer. Saying a prayer together, such as the Lord's Prayer, brings your hearts and voices together in prayer. The goal of praying together as a family is not to pray in a correct way or to force each person to say something. The goal is to experience God's presence as a family.

Creating a place where each family member can write a prayer for everyone to read and pray on his or her behalf teaches children the importance of intercessory prayer. Children come to know that others are praying for them, and that they are praying for others as well. At my home we write our prayers in a small sandbox, erasing the prayers after a time with a tiny rake. Someone might write, "Help me with my math test." Or someone might write the name of an ill family member or draw a symbol such as a sad face. Whenever we see the message in the sandbox, we pause and pray.

> **Praying at home . . . will not happen if we do not have set times to pray together as families.**

3. Encourage Children to Pray on Their Own

In addition to praying together as a family, it is important to assist and encourage children to pray on their own. The best way to ensure that children will make prayer part of their life is for them to see their parents authentically praying. Make prayer a part of your vocabulary. Tell your children what you are praying for and when your prayers are answered. As you are tucking them into bed, pray over them and for them. Later in your children's lives, they will remember seeing you pray and will be more likely to pray on a regular basis.

Children pray differently according to their ages, verbal skills, and attitudes toward prayer. Some children who are extroverts will be willing to pray aloud, whereas more introverted children will want their prayer times to be more private. Young children usually are more willing to share their prayers than teens. That is okay. Don't assume your child is not praying because he or she isn't sharing every word and phrase of every prayer with you.

The best way to ensure that children will make prayer part of their life is for them to see their parents authentically praying.

Prayer is spending time in the presence of God. This can happen in a variety of ways—with and without words. Here are some examples of different ways to teach children to pray.

Breath Prayer

One of the simplest prayers to teach children is the breath prayer. This prayer simply allows children to connect to God through their breathing. As they breathe in deeply and slowly, they breathe in the light and love and holiness of God. As they breathe out, they give to God any worries, fears, and concerns. Giving a child a pinwheel or some bubbles to use while doing the breath prayer can serve as a reminder to pray.

Whole Body Prayers

Whole body prayers are another powerful kind of prayer. Play music and allow children to dance or move as they pray. This helps them use their whole bodies in prayer. Older children might enjoy using their whole bodies to grow and tend a garden, asking God to tend to their prayer requests, needs, and worries as they tend to their plants. Taking a walk together and looking for signs of God's presence is another form of whole body prayer.

Contemplative Prayer

Contemplative prayer is prayer without words when we sit quietly and listen to God. Give your child an electric candle or crayons and paper and instruct the child to sit quietly and reflect and pray in silence. This will help to teach your child to listen to God.

Praying With Words

Praying with words involves spoken prayers, such as mealtime and bedtime prayers and saying the Lord's Prayer together. Praying with words also can include writing or drawing in a journal and using flashcards with words on them to create personalized prayers. Encouraging children to use their own words is an important step in helping them know that they can express themselves to God and that prayer is not about using the correct form but about speaking to God in whatever form we choose.

The work you do to create a home filled with prayer will matter to your children.

Prayer Reminders

Prayer reminders are items or symbols children can wear or display that remind them to pray. Jesus wore a prayer shawl and touched a *mezuzah* each time he left or came into his house. These were prayer reminders. Hanging a small cross on the doorknob of your home will remind children that they belong to God each time they open the door. Giving them a special bracelet or necklace to wear reminds them that God is with them at all times and they can turn to God in prayer whenever they need or want.

4. Make Prayer a Regular Part of Family Life

The important thing about praying at home is not how you do it, how long you do it, or even how often you do it. The important thing is simply that you make prayer a regular part of your family's life together.

My family used to pray together each Sunday night. Following our Sunday night dinner, we would light sacred candles, read the Bible together, say the Lord's Prayer, and sit quietly for a few moments, simply being in the presence of God. We did this for several years. On many nights my kids would complain about our prayer time because they wanted get started on their homework or watch a television show. Sometimes they would act silly during the quiet time. Many nights I wondered why I was even trying to have prayer time because of their attitudes. But I believed it was important, so I kept doing it.

On September 11, 2001, when the planes flew into the World Trade Center in New York City, I heard my son, who was in the sixth grade at the time, doing something in the kitchen. I thought he was getting himself breakfast. But then he came back into the living room. He had our sacred candles, the ones we lit each Sunday night, in his hands. He set them on each side of our television and lit them. We said no words, but the lighting of the candles was our family prayer, and I knew that all the work I had done encouraging my family to pray had mattered. The work you do to create a home filled with prayer will matter to your children, as well!

Ideas to Consider

- If prayer in the home is equally important as prayer in the church, what role should the church play in equipping and assisting families to pray together?
- Why is it helpful to provide families with different prayer forms and tools? How might you do this?
- Prayer reminders can be helpful tools for encouraging prayer. What are the "prayer reminders" in your church? How might you encourage families to create and use their own prayer reminders?
- The story about lighting the prayer candles on September 11, 2001, is a moving example of the power of regular times of family prayer. How might you gather and share other stories about family prayer experiences to encourage families in your congregation?

WHAT IS PRAYER, REALLY?

Andy Langford

How do we define prayer? Prayer is a way of living every moment of every day with the possibility of being in communication with God. Better than a cell phone or beeper, God is always accessible to people who pray. The word "prayer" means to petition or to beg. Prayer is sharing with God the most needful parts of our life, begging for guidance, and then listening for God's answer. Through prayer we have an immediate, one-on-one communication with God; and in the community of faith, the prayers of the whole community shout out for God's attention.

Prayer is not a form of spiritual bargaining in which our community of faith gains control over God and somehow directs God's bidding. In such cases, prayer could become an invoice that God is obliged to pay. Nor is prayer a kind of spiritual aerobics—an activity that may strengthen the faith of those who pray but have no effect on God. In this case, prayer is like going to the gym, giving us only personal benefits such as calmness. To say that prayer always changes God is to say too much. To say that prayer only changes us is to say too little.

PRAYING COUPLES

Laurie Lowe Barnes

Laurie Lowe Barnes *is ustor of Bristol Hill United Methodist Church in Cansas City, Kansas. Previ- usly she served as Pastor of Prayer and Congregational Care at The United Methodist Church of the Resurrection in Leawood, Kansas. In this article she presents the concept of a lass designed to teach and encourage couples to pray ogether on a regular basis.*

What can happen in just five minutes a day? Quite a lot when it comes to prayer!

About a year ago, prayer ministry volunteer Shirley Yarick and I developed a two-week class called Couples in Prayer. Our goal was to encourage couples to pray out loud together five minutes a day for fifteen days. We hoped that by encouraging couples to perse-vere for more than two weeks, we would help couples to establish a habit of praying together that would con-tinue throughout the rest of their lives.

Inspiration for this project came when pastor Adam Hamilton and his wife, LaVon, led a marriage-themed cruise to Alaska with couples from the United Methodist Church of the Resurrection in Leawood, Kansas. While leading that cruise, one of the Hamil-tons' first discoveries was that many of the couples did not practice the spiritual discipline of regularly pray-ing together. They found that both individuals in the marriage rela-tionship tended to pray individually

Praying together on a regular basis strengthens the bonds of love and respect between a couple.

on a regular basis, but rarely did they pray together as a couple. Adam and LaVon knew from personal experience that praying together on a regular basis strengthens the bonds of love and respect between a couple. Furthermore, they recognized that communicating together on a regular basis with God has a pos-itive effect on communicating with a spouse or relationship partner. So, after returning from the cruise, Adam asked the prayer ministry at Church of the Resurrection to develop a class to teach and encourage couples to pray together on a regular basis.

Communicating together on a regular basis with God has a positive effect on communicating with a spouse or relationship partner.

The first class began a few months later with twenty couples. Five min-utes a day seemed a doable period of time for couples to get started in this prayer experiment. But would it last? As time passed, a number of the couples reported that this time together was making a difference, and they have continued in prayer as a couple. One couple shared these comments:

> *The initial five minutes is usually not enough now. We find the time together is a great way to connect, review the day, outline our prayer requests, and look for answered prayers. We also pray for each other, frequently asking God to help us with issues that, unless discussed in "prayer mode," might be interpreted as confrontational. This has nearly eliminated the need for discussions regarding any problems we are having. These discussions were few in number anyway, but they are even fewer now that we go to God in prayer as a couple.*

We began each class with the Couples in Prayer Covenant on page 177. Session plans and other resources for the two-week course are provided on the accompanying DVD-Rom.

Ideas to Consider

- Conduct a survey among married couples in your church to determine how many pray together on a regular basis. Are you surprised by your findings?
- Why do you think most couples do not practice the spiritual discipline of regularly praying together?
- What are the benefits of couples praying together regularly?
- Who in your congregation might help to plan and/or lead a class to teach and encourage couples to pray together? What steps do you need to take to get the process in motion?

Couples in Prayer Covenant

We accept the challenge of praying together for five minutes a day for the next fifteen days to form the habit of praying together as a couple. We believe this will strengthen our marriage and/or our relationship because we are making God our partner. We accept that this is not an opportunity to discuss potential areas of improvement but, instead, is an intimate and special time together.

As participants we will:
• Strive to honor God through daily prayer;
• Pray regularly together as a couple;
• Pray to have open hearts and minds as to what God will teach about prayer;
• Be faithful to read Scripture in order to know more about God and what God expects of us; and
• Respect privacy and intimacy with each other.

Our time and place to pray will be:

_____

_____   _____
Signed   Signed

Date_____

Therefore a man leaves his father and his mother and clings to his wife, and they become one flesh. (Genesis 2:24)

PARENTS TEACHING CHILDREN TO PRAY

Steve Richards

Steve Richards *and his wife, Amanda, are the parents of two daughters. Currently, he serves as pastor of Messiah United Methodist Church in Plymouth, Minnesota. In this article, adapted from the* **FaithHome for Parents** *series (Abingdon, 1999), Steve explores how to teach children the basics of prayer.*

Lauren climbed into bed, and I tucked her in. As I sat down on the edge of the bed, I said, "Are you ready to say a prayer?"

"Dear God," Lauren began, "thank you for Mommy and Daddy and Bethany. Thank you for all good things. Help Grandma get well, and help me feel better about school. Watch over everyone tonight. Amen."

I remember that night as if it was yesterday, and I remember just as vividly my own childhood ritual of bedtime prayer. Every night my mother and I would talk about the activities of the day before saying a bedtime prayer. My childhood prayers were much the same as the prayer spoken by my daughter Lauren: both included the significant people in our lives. As a father, I have learned what my mother also learned as she sat on my bed listening to her child pray: our children's thoughts and the yearnings of their hearts are expressed in their prayers. As I listened to my daughter's prayer that night, I heard the concerns that she had carried through the day. Her prayer gave me a glimpse of her needs and her trust that God was with her as her friend.

Prayer: The Language of the Heart

Prayer is the language of the heart. Whether the language is spoken or remains silent, prayer allows us to express our inner thoughts and emotions. Prayer also provides a means for us to support others—even those persons we have never met. Prayer is our special connection with God.

Prayer is an ongoing conversation and growing friendship with God through words and thoughts. When we pray with our children, we are sharing the relationship we have with God at the same time we are expressing our love for our children.

How to Teach a Child to Pray

1. Begin where the child is.

It is never too early or too late to teach your child to pray. With an infant, you can begin by singing "Jesus Loves Me" and speaking simple words of thanks for your child—such as, "Thank you, God, for Kyle." With an older child, pause at mealtime and bedtime to say a few words of thanks for the meal and the day.

Prayers of thanks are a good way to teach children to pray; even very young children can name things for which they are thankful. Using your child's name in your own prayers of thanks will teach your child that she or he is important to God. Your child can begin to experience a relationship with God without having to understand that relationship. As a parent, you want your child to know that God is personal. God is ready to hear the words of even the youngest child, because God is present with each of us.

2. Establish a regular pattern of prayer.

Children learn through ritual and routine. Mealtime and bedtime are two good occasions for establishing a ritual.

Saying a prayer before a meal reminds a child that we are part of the world God has made, and that we are grateful for the food we need in order to live. You may want to use the same prayer before each meal, find several prayers from which to choose, create a new prayer each time, or have each person share a Bible verse. Hold hands around the table or fold your hands as the prayer is said by one or by all.

Bedtime has always been our family's time to quiet ourselves and prayerfully reflect on the day. As you help your child get ready for bed, let this be a time to give thanks and pray for each other.

Look for other times and ways to make prayer a regular part of your family's life together. Your child will begin to anticipate your special prayer rituals and may even remind you when it's time to pray!

3. Help your child to memorize some simple prayers.

Teaching children some simple prayers they can recite from memory helps ease them into the practice of prayer. Say the prayers aloud with your child to help him or her feel relaxed and confident. Work on learning one prayer, repeating it until your child has memorized it. Then begin working on another prayer. Start simple and work up to longer, more difficult prayers as your child is ready.

There are many wonderful collections of children's prayers from which to choose, including some beautifully illustrated books that you can enjoy together.

When your child is ready for longer prayers, include the Lord's Prayer. Jesus offered this prayer as an example of how we are to pray (Luke 11:1-4). It contains specific guidelines for prayer: praise, thanks, forgiveness, and direction. Children do not need to fully understand the words in order to memorize the prayer. In fact, even four- and five-year-olds have been known to master this prayer in a relatively short time.

4. Model prayer for your child.

Children learn the importance of prayer by watching and listening as their parents pray. We adults look forward to hearing children pray, but it is important for children to know that prayer isn't just for kids. Pray daily for your child. Pray daily with your child. Allow your child to see the importance of prayer in your own life.

Prayer can include:
Worship—recognizing the glory and power of God
Confession—confessing and asking forgiveness for wrong behavior
Thanks—giving thanks for what you have, for family, home, friends
Asking—asking help and blessings for self and others
Listening—taking time to be still and listen to God's word in your heart

What to Teach a Child About Prayer

1. Prayer is simply talking with God.

Children need to know that they can talk to God just as they would talk to a parent or a good friend—wherever and whenever they want. God is always ready to listen. Look for opportunities to offer simple, spontaneous prayers in the presence of your child—such as thanking God for a beautiful sunset, expressing your concern for sick friend or pet, asking for God's help with a particular problem or situation, or thanking God for the gift of your child. The best way to teach your child to pray is by your own example.

2. Prayer involves listening as well as speaking.

The psalmist writes, "Be still, and know that I am God" (Psalm 46:10). For a conversation to be meaningful, someone must be listening. Prayer is our conversation with God. If our prayers are to be meaningful, we must listen to God.

Being quiet and listening do not come naturally for many children. As a child, I tried to follow the long prayers of the Sunday worship service, but usually my mind would wander and I would think about the people and things important to me. Yet because of what I had learned about prayer, I knew that God was with me when I prayed. I knew that prayer was my special time alone with God. I believed it was the time when God was thinking about me.

How can you begin to teach your child that prayer involves listening as well as talking? First, find ways to introduce the concept of listening and help your child practice listening, such as spending quiet time together, listening to quiet music together, reading to your child, and so forth.

Help your child understand that prayer does not have to be spoken. Ask your child to draw a picture of things for which he or she is thankful or persons he or she loves. Some of the most meaningful "prayers" I have witnessed were drawn by a child.

When praying with your child, ask your child to think quietly about God and the questions he or she has for God.

Take a walk outside and ask your child to listen quietly to all the sounds of God's creation. Then have your child identify as many of those sounds as he or she can. Talk about how we can hear (and see) God in the world around us.

3. God answers prayer, but not always in the ways we want or expect.

The more we pray, the easier it becomes—and the better we become at "hearing God," and at recognizing God's answers to our prayers. God does answer our prayers, but not always how or when we want or expect. Sometimes we pray for healing for someone who does not get better. Sometimes we ask for something that never happens or that we never receive. Explaining this concept to young children can be difficult. The best approach is to keep it simple. Assure your child that although we may not always understand the things that happen and why God chooses to act or not to act in certain ways, we can be sure of God's love for us (Romans 8:38-39) and God's promise to be with us always (Matthew 28:20b).

Prayer takes patience and persistence. In time we learn to listen not for what we want, but for what God wants, trusting that God will always be with us and will help us in ways we may not be able to see or fully understand.

Ideas to Consider

- If you are a parent of young children, have you established a regular practice of prayer with your child/children? If not, consider some times you and your child/children could devote to prayer daily.
- Remember that the best way to teach a child to pray is by your own example.

VI.
LIVING AS A PRAYING CONGREGATION

Prayer is indeed a way of living. *Becoming a Praying Congregation* is designed to bring this way of living to reality in the life and ministry of your congregation. Establishing a new way of living isn't a task that can be accomplished by one or two people in response to a sermon or a class or a new book. This real and growing companionship with God is a lifelong journey for each individual, family, and congregation. This section provides practical tools for sustaining and enriching the journey through the first twelve months and beyond. As you explore ways your congregation may maintain enthusiasm and build momentum, consider the following:

- What are some of the potential challenges we face as we seek to sustain a yearlong emphasis on prayer?
- How can we utilize existing methods of communication to hold interest and maintain focus?
- How can we target specific groups and segments within the congregation in our planning, communication, and implementation of activities and events?
- How will we handle discouragement or uncertainty regarding the impact we are having?
- How can we help our congregation to continue growing and maturing in a life of prayer after the first twelve months?

Articles:

183

SUSTAINING A PRAYING CONGREGATION THROUGH THE FIRST YEAR

Like any journey, living as a praying congregation requires time and effort. The process is not self-sustaining but requires intentionality and ongoing attention. Maintaining enthusiasm and building momentum involve planning and work. To hold interest and focus throughout the first year, look for ways to use existing methods of communicating with the congregation. Here are some ideas to get you started:

Worship

- Announce the prayer emphasis, as well as specific activities and events, in worship through the use of the bulletin, slide projection, and spoken announcements. (See bulletin ideas below.)
- Create colorful banners or other visual displays related to the emphasis or to prayer in general and display them in the sanctuary—either throughout the year or on designated Sundays (e.g., the first Sunday of every month).
- Introduce a new prayer practice, preferably without any announcement or explanation, and continue it week to week, (e.g., a moment of silence).
- Explore ways to make prayer more meaningful during worship.
- Plan a 4–6-week sermon series on prayer—at least once and perhaps twice during the year.
- Hold a special prayer service. (See "Special Events" on page 186.)
- Have key leaders share testimonials in worship related to prayer and their experiences using *When You Pray*.

Bulletin / Newsletter / Website

- Share quotes or excerpts from *When You Pray* and *Becoming a Praying Congregation* on a regular basis. Formatted quotes are available on the DVD-Rom. Note: Fair use allows you to print up to 300 words from a copyrighted source without obtaining permission from the publisher. Please include the following credit lines:

  From *When You Pray*, by Rueben P. Job (Abingdon Press, 2009); p. __.
  From *Becoming a Praying Congregation* (Abingdon Press, 2009); p. __.

- Address a "Question of the Week/Month" pertaining to prayer.
- Create a logo or special design to use in conjunction with "Becoming a Praying Congregation" or other catch phrase or slogan. Use this on all

printed materials as well as on your website whenever making announcements or sharing any information related to the prayer emphasis.

- Include articles on prayer and/or short testimonials from leaders and members related to prayer and their experiences using *When You Pray*.
- Provide links on your website to other helpful sites pertaining to the practice of prayer. (Be sure to include links that will meet the needs of individuals, children and youth, and families.)

Special Events
- Plan a special prayer service or event. Make this an occasional or regular occurrence.
- Use familiar as well as new prayer practices. Perhaps plan a special event to introduce a new prayer practice.
- Hold special events for children and/or youth, or invite them to lead a prayer event for the congregation.
- Ask individuals and families to share their experiences in a celebratory prayer event.

In addition to utilizing communication tools that reach the entire congregation, target specific segments and groups within the congregation—such as children and youth, singles, young adults, men's and women's groups, seniors, recovery or support groups, specific committees or teams, and so forth. Ask yourself questions such as these:

- How can we invite this group to participate in planned activities, studies, or other events?
- How can we involve them in planning and leading specific activities or events?
- How can we assist or equip this group as they seek to develop a life of prayer?

To illustrate, here are some ideas for small groups, committees, and new members. Perhaps these ideas will serve as a springboard for creating your own ideas for other segments and groups within your congregation:

Small Groups and Committees
- Encourage leadership committees/groups to use *When You Pray* in their personal prayer practice throughout the year.
- Encourage all committees to open their meetings with prayer and worship.
- Invite existing Sunday school classes and other small groups to use *When You Pray* and *When You Pray as a Small Group* for a short-term or ongoing study emphasis.
- Launch one or more new groups using these resources.

New Members
- Provide every new member with a copy of *When You Pray* (or another prayer guide) and encourage them to use it regularly to begin or renew a personal prayer practice.
- As new people join the congregation, they will look for ways to connect with the culture of your church. Joining a group in covenant for daily prayer is a significant way to meet and connect. Establish a group of long-time members who meet together to share Scripture and prayer and who are prepared to welcome and bring in new members through the year. Or, arrange for existing prayer groups to be ready to welcome new members. Joining a group can introduce your new members to a transforming way of engaging Scripture and prayer.

RE-LAUNCHING A PRAYER EMPHASIS MIDYEAR

All journeys have starts and stops of one kind or another, and you may find that your journey toward a more vital prayer life in your congregation has similar ups and downs. At any point, you can regroup your leadership team, re-assess, look through the various activity ideas for the year, and begin again. One of the most effective ways to sustain the journey for your congregation is simply to regroup and start afresh.

At the beginning of this book, you read that "we cannot be spiritual leaders without the Spirit's help." In your own companionship with God in Christ, you are continually formed and fed for ministry. Likewise, if you should become discouraged or your team become unsure of whether or not they are making an impact, a renewed collective investment in prayer is a great way to discern your next steps. As you prayerfully consider how to re-launch your prayer emphasis, consider the following suggestions and how you might adapt them to fit your particular congregation:

Prayer Event

A special prayer event is a great way to re-launch a congregational prayer emphasis any time momentum is slowing. Halfway through the first year is generally a good marker as well. Have your leadership team or worship team plan the event. Here are just a few possible ideas:

- *24-hour Prayer-a-thon* – Have individuals sign up for 15–30-minute intervals. Create a prayerful atmosphere in the sanctuary or other location and provide brief instructions for participants to read as they arrive.
- *Prayer Service* – Structure the service however you wish, allowing time for as few or as many various forms of prayer as you like, such as collects, responsive readings, sharing of prayer requests, pastoral prayer, silent prayer, spontaneous prayer, sung prayer (solos and/or unison singing). You might consider inviting leaders, individuals, and families from the congregation to share their experiences thus far in developing a life of prayer.
- *Labyrinth* – The prayer labyrinth is one of the oldest contemplative tools known for meditating, praying, and connecting with God. Long ago, prayer labyrinths were considered and even modeled to be a journey to Jerusalem, the center of the world. A prayer labyrinth has one path, serving as a powerful symbol of an individual's life journey and

pilgrimage of faith. Create a prayer labyrinth on church property and open it to all individuals, families, or groups seeking contemplation and prayer. You will find one prayer labyrinth model on the DVD-Rom.

Intergenerational Prayer Activity

- Plan a prayer exercise that reaches across generations. An ideal time for such an activity is Advent or Lent, although you may plan this kind of prayer activity anytime you need to re-start your prayer emphasis. A short-term intergenerational activity might invite families to begin a season of prayers at home following *When You Pray* or *When You Pray as a Family*. Or invite children and youth teams to write original prayers for the season and share at a special midweek evening meal.
- An intergenerational prayer activity is an excellent way to involve youth in the congregational prayer emphasis. Consider having the youth plan and lead the event, soliciting help and participation from the entire congregation.
- Have a prayer walk for the youth. Each youth starts off along a path at timed intervals. As the youth walks, he or she encounters older adults who have been stationed along the path to talk and pray with the youth related to specific, pre-assigned topics. You could plan a similar prayer walk for children, individuals, couples, or entire families.
- Host a labyrinth prayer walk on Christmas Eve or Good Friday. Some denominational offices have portable labyrinths on canvas or you might trace the art provided on the accompanying DVD-Rom.

Mission-Oriented Prayer Focus

- Connect your prayer focus to a specific mission or outreach activity or effort. For example, if your church is sponsoring a mission trip, recruit volunteers to pray for purpose of the trip, the participants, and those you'll visit. If you have a seasonal mission activity, include requests for prayers for the planning and work of the team. Churches could sponsor personal one-on-one prayers for community first responders, like paramedics, police officers, and firefighters. A group might work with the city to pray for specific individuals.

LIVING AS A PRAYING CONGREGATION AFTER THE FIRST YEAR

Becoming a Praying Congregation is designed not only to be a twelve-month congregational focus but also an ongoing journey. After the first year, you can help your congregation to continue growing and maturing in a life of prayer by providing new experiences, activities, and resources that encourage the practice of prayer. Here are just a few ideas and resources you might consider:

Other Resources on Prayer

A Guide to Prayer for All Who Seek God, Norman Shawchuck and Rueben P. Job (Upper Room Books, 2006)

This guide offers a daily pattern for those seeking a rhythm of devotion and personal worship. Following the Christian year and the lectionary readings, each day offers guidance for an opening affirmation, a petition of prayer, and daily Scripture selections.

See also *A Guide to Prayer for All God's People* (Upper Room, 1990) and *A Guide to Prayer for Ministers and Other Servants* (Upper Room, 1991).

A Guide to Retreat for All God's Shepherds, Rueben P. Job (Abingdon Press, 1994)

This guide is designed to assist pastors and leaders in a time of reflection, prayer, and renewal. The resources included are intended to help individuals turn more fully toward God, to think more deeply about God, and to prepare themselves for faithful ministry.

A Wesleyan Spiritual Reader, Rueben P. Job (Abingdon, 1998)

This book provides resources for a 26-week devotional experience involving daily prayer and reflection. The volume includes Scripture, spiritual readings (primarily quotes from the writings of John Wesley), and an essay by the author.

Companions in Christ: The Way of Prayer, Jane Vennard and Stephen Bryant (Upper Room, 2007)

The Way of Prayer expands on our knowledge of prayer through a ten-week exploration of different forms of prayer practices. Through this exploration, small-group members discover different dimensions of God's grace and love. Prayer is explored through music, dance, gazing, silence, or acts of service. *The Way of Prayer* teaches us how to respond to God's invitation into the divine Presence and brings a deeper sense of spiritual vitality and encouragement to seek out new ways to pray.

***The Awkward Season: Prayers for Lent*, Pamela Hawkins (Upper Room, 2009)**

This book offers Christian pilgrims a "prayer path" to follow through Lent. For each day of the week, prayers of invocation, confession, and thanksgiving are shaped around a theme promoted by the psalm for the day. A daily Scripture reading is provided, but flexibility is offered. This book is designed to support rather than dictate a Lenten journey.

***The Workbook of Living Prayer*, Maxie Dunnam (Upper Room, 1994)**

This six-week prayer adventure features daily commentary on a particular facet of prayer, Scripture readings, and reflections by the author.

***Fifty Ways to Pray: Traditions From Many Traditions and Times*, Teresa Blythe (Abingdon, 2006)**

Each of the exercises includes instructions on how it can be used as a prayer practice, but also provides some background, an introduction, a statement of intention, and tips to help you become comfortable with the practice. Also included are special instructions and information in the Leader's Guide at the end of the book.

Guest Speakers

Invite a guest speaker to kick off the next year of your church's prayer ministry/focus. Leaders from other denominations or faith traditions may be able to offer fresh insights on their own prayer traditions.

Start New Small Groups

The small-group experience is the ideal environment for teaching, modeling, and perfecting a life of prayer. Form a new group to study one of the previously suggested prayer resources, or suggest existing groups choose one resource from the list to study sometime during the next year. Ask participants from ongoing groups to share about their experience of prayer in small groups. Some members who were not ready or able to join a group previously may join now.

Annual or Seasonal "Family Prayer" Kickoff

To encourage families to continue the practice of prayer at home, host an annual "Family Prayer Kickoff." Remind families of the importance and benefits of praying together, share experiences and celebrate accomplishments from the previous year and provide instruction through small groups and/or activities. Consider serving a meal or snack and including some fun family games or activities.

SOURCES

[1] Rhor, Richard. *Everything Belongs* (Crossroad Publishing Company); p. 29.

[2] Brame, Grace Adolphsen. *Receptive Prayer* (CBP Press, 1985); p. 9.

[3] Wesley, John. "Journal From August 12, 1738, to November 1, 1739," Vol. 1; p. 161.

[4] Wesley, John. "Letters to Mr. John Trembath," Vol. 12; p. 254.

[5] Thompson, Marjorie J. *Soulfeast: An Invitation to the Christian Spiritual Life* (Westminster John Knox, 2005); p. 33.

[6] Thompson; p. 33.

[7] Brueggemann, Walter. *Awed to Heaven, Rooted in Earth* (Augsburg Fortress, 2003); p. xvi.

[8] Phifer, Kenneth G. *A Book of Uncommon Prayer* (Upper Room Books, 1981); p. 34.

[9] Scifres, Mary J. and B. J. Beu, eds. *The Abingdon Worship Annual 2005: Contemporary and Traditional Resources for Worship Leaders* (Abingdon Press, 2004); p. 10.

[10] Nouwen, Henri J. M. *The Only Necessary Thing: Living a Prayerful Life* (Crossroad, 1999); p. 123.

[11] Scifres and Beu, eds.; p. 10.

[12] Fosdick, Harry Emerson. *A Book of Public Prayers* (Harper & Brothers, 1959); pp. 30–31.

[13] From "Wesley's Covenant Service" in *The United Methodist Book of Worship* (The United Methodist Publishing House, 1992); p. 291. See also *When You Pray*, by Rueben P. Job (Abingdon Press, 2009); p. 24.

[14] Here, editor Grace Adolphsen Brame summarizes Evelyn Underhill's point from one of Underhill's retreats, compiled in *The Ways of the Spirit* (Crossroad, 1993); pp. 22, 77.

[15] Wesley, John. "Letters to Mr. John Trembath," Vol. 12; p. 254.,

[16] Yancey, Philip. *Prayer: Does It Make Any Difference?* (Zondervan, 2006); p. 55.

[17] Yancey; p. 226.

[18] Dunnam, Maxie. *The Workbook of Living Prayer* (Upper Room, 1994); pp. 98–99. Retrieved from *The Workbook of Living Prayer* by Maxie Dunnam ©1994 by Upper Room Books®. Used by permission from Upper Room Books®. To order, phone 1.800.972.0433 or www.upperroom.org/bookstore.

[19] Yancey; p. 139.

[20] Job, Rueben P. *When You Pray: Daily Practices for Prayerful Living* (Abingdon Press, 2009); pp. 85–86.

[21] Job; pp. 45–46.

[22] Steere, Douglas V. *Dimensions of Prayer: Cultivating a Relationship With God* (Upper Room Books, 1997); pp. 98–99.

[23] Wren, Brian. *What Language Shall I Borrow?* (Crossroad, 1989); p. 5.

[24] Nouwen, *The Only Necessary Thing*; p. 127.

[25] Nouwen, Henri J. M. *Ministry and Spirituality* (Continuum, 1996); p. 280.

[26] Yancey; p. 112.

[27] Wesley, John. Sermon 16 "The Means of Grace," Vol. 5; pp. 187–188.)

[28] Wesley, John. "A Plain Account of Christian Perfection," Vol. 11; p. 437. Original phrasing, "God does nothing but in answer to prayer."

[29] Galli, Mark and James S. Bell, Jr. *The Complete Idiot's Guide to Prayer* (Alpha, 2004); p. 137.

[30] *Many Thoughts of Many Minds: A Treasury of Quotations From the Literature of Every Land and Every Age* (Hard Press, 2006); p. 179.

[31] Bell, Jr., James S. and Tracy Macon Sumner. *The Complete Idiot's Guide to Christian Prayers & Devotions* (Alpha, 2007); p. 186.

[32] Quoted in *The Way of the Heart*, by Henri J. M. Nouwen (HarperOne, 1991); p. 76.

[33] Cloyd, Betty Shannon. *Children and Prayer: A Shared Pilgrimage* (Upper Room, 1997); p. 24.

[34] Pipher, Mary. *The Shelter of Each Other* (Ballantine Books, 1996); p. 59.

[35] de Caussade, Jean-Pierre. *Abandonment to Divine Providence* (Dover, 2008).